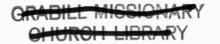

It Began With An Island

Sandy Barker

THOMAS NELSON PUBLISHERS
Nashville • Camden • New York

Contents

ONE

Senior Blues

As I walked back across campus to my apartment that cold, rainy September day, my mood was as stormy as the Knoxville sky. Eat, sleep, study, work; eat, sleep, study, work. My steps echoed the monotonous beat of my hectic daily routine. I juggled the books in my arms to look at my watch. Only thirty minutes to eat and catch the bus to work.

I trudged on toward the railroad tracks, staring ahead at the steep bank I climbed each day to get home. *If it weren't for Joe I probably wouldn't even be at the University of Tennessee*, I thought. I longed to see him, but that was impossible. He was four thousand miles away, and I had only his letters to keep me going.

A train whistle jolted my thoughts, and I fell backward down the muddy bank. My books slid along the wet grass. Tears filled my eyes. "You're crazy," I said to myself. "You almost got hit by a train, and all you can think of is Joe!"

I made my way on up the slippery bank and jogged across the parking lot to my mailbox. I spun the combination lock quickly. Got one! I tore it open as I pulled it from the box, hoping the news was good. Four thousand miles is a long way for two people who have no official commitments to each other.

> Sandy, I'm running an ad in the newspaper here to buy a small island in Lake Nicaragua. The islands are beautiful—swaying palms, mango trees, and waves lapping at the rocks. I advertised for one about an acre in size, and they are so cheap that I really think I could get exactly what I want for about forty-five hundred dollars. I have maps of them and they're perfect. Sandy, I know all this sounds a little far out. . . .

Now, I knew Joe was a dreamer, but after reading that letter, I thought, *He's gone crazy! An island?* There I was, going to school full-time, working full-time, and not even knowing why, and the guy I'd fallen in love with was wanting to buy an island!

A tiny piece of newsprint fluttered to the ground. It was the ad, in Spanish.

Why had he gone back to Nicaragua, anyway? Why couldn't he be like other architecture students who went down for one quarter and then came back home to stay?

Nine months before, I had never even heard of Nicaragua.

The earthquake—that's what had started the whole crazy idea. A disaster four thousand miles away had affected our lives here in Tennessee.

Seeing the destruction of Managua, Nicaragua, on December 23, 1972, Joe's professor, Dr. Joseph Kersavage, had also seen an opportunity for his architecture students. They could get practical experience and at the same time offer much-needed assistance to the government of Nicaragua.

Arrangements had been made: Nicaragua would provide room and board, and the UT School of Architecture would give credit to any students who qualified.

Joe and eight other students had been developing light-weight roofing systems and had won the Reynolds Aluminum Student Competition for an innovative use of aluminum screen wire. In Nicaragua, where heavy tile roofs had caved in and killed so many people, the utility of the system would be apparent.

On New Year's Day, 1974, Dr. K's group had set out from Knoxville in two University vans and headed south on Interstate 75 to cross five national borders. For the next three months, Joe had written about their adventures driving through Mexico, the warm reception in Nicaragua, and the beautiful people they had tried to help.

Joe did return to Knoxville for course work that late March, but when it was completed, he had returned to Managua in August. That second good-by had been painful.

Now, this letter telling me about his dream to buy an island.

I guess I'll just go on working at Tennessee School for the Deaf once I graduate in June, I thought, staring at Joe's letter. I enjoyed my recreation work at TSD, but what I really wanted—more than anything else—was to be with Joe.

For the past year, I hadn't even noticed anyone else. I'd met Joe at a wedding, and if there is such thing as love at first sight, then that's what had happened to me.

I had been attending a Bible college at the time, and Joe had been in a rock band. I guess we surprised each other; I wasn't a prude, and he wasn't a maniac. When we had held hands, fireworks had gone off inside—a new response for both of us. We had spent weekends sailing his homemade sailboat and sharing our dreams with each other. Then the opportunity for Joe to go to Nicaragua had come. It was his brass ring, and he had to grab it.

I had transferred to UT and waited for him to return in March. From April through August we had relished every possible moment together between classes and work. Then he had left for Nicaragua again, leaving me to face my senior classes at UT alone.

When we had said good-by, I could never have guessed that Joe's crazy dreams would become mine and that I would soon be building a house and a life in Nicaragua with him.

Throughout the fall of 1974, Joe continued to write more tantalizing information about the islands. His next letter steamed with excitement.

> These islands are only five miles from a big city called Granada where I could work. It is only forty miles to Managua from Granada. The lake is one hundred miles long and thirty-seven miles wide, so it is like an ocean with volcanic islands and fresh-water sharks! People are already living in beautiful houses on some of the islands.
>
> This weekend I am chartering a boat to go out and cruise around the islands. There must be about three hundred of them, but they're far enough apart that I can still run around naked. I want an island with nothing on it but trees. People are anxious to sell land for enough money to start rebuilding after the earthquake.

One day, not long after that letter had arrived, I was summoned to the door from my sociology class by an architecture student. The first thought that entered my mind was, *Oh, no, something has happened to Joe.* I could just imagine another earthquake. I remembered the pictures Joe had shown me of the pile of rubble that had once been a city. Thousands of people had been buried alive. My heart pounded.

The student held out a slip of paper. "Are you Joe Barker's girlfriend?"

"Yes," I answered weakly. "What's happened?"

"Dean Hanson told me to find you and tell you that Joe has to register in order to graduate this quarter."

"What?" I practically screamed. "This is the middle of the quarter! What are you talking about?"

"Evidently, Joe had some parking tickets he never paid, so the admissions office won't process his registration. Can you take care of it for him?"

A mixed flood of anger and relief welled up inside me. Joe was safe. But now I was going to have to walk all over campus doing his paper work while he discovered a dreamy tropical paradise!

Two days later I had straightened out the mess. Joe would graduate in December 1974. I allowed myself to chastise him in my next letter.

Meanwhile Joe kept writing about the islands. One unforgettable October day my spirits soared as I read:

> Honey, all this sounds like a dream, but I know we can buy our very own island. From our island we could sail straight to the Caribbean and anywhere in the world.
>
> I miss you more than ever, especially now that I really feel we can do this. Today I could just picture you sitting in the hammock with me and hugging me as we watched the sun set over the water. It won't be long before we can do just that. . . .

As I stood looking down from my apartment toward the Tennessee River, his letter seemed just too good to be true. Now he was using the words *our* and *we*. I held my breath as I gazed out at the flaming colors of the trees along the river's edge.

I looked toward the sky and breathed a prayer, "O, God, please let it be so. Let this be the real thing. I ask You to show me Your will about everything. I pray in Jesus' name, amen."

I looked down at the letter in my hand. "I love you." *I love you*, he had written. I started to believe that perhaps we would really be together.

But the days dragged on. I remember one letter that came when I was really feeling low:

Sandy, I have never in my life seen a sunset like this. How could anyone doubt God? And it's free. Next door, people are running around a wooden shack with a dirt floor. But they get front row seats to a show like this.

What a romantic!

Joe said that U.S. diplomas were highly respected in Nicaragua. I laughed to think that I was getting my degree in health, P.E., and recreation and might end up living on an island. What better place to recreate?

The last two weeks of the quarter were a blur. My calendar says I had four exams, a research paper, and a report due, but I don't remember any of it. After all my weeks of waiting, writing, and hoping, Joe was finally coming home!

As he stepped off the plane that cold December night, I hardly recognized him. He had grown a beard, his hair was shaggy, and he was deeply tanned.

Palms sweaty, heart beating rapidly, I walked hesitantly toward him, fighting the nagging fear that perhaps his feelings had changed as much as his appearance.

Then our eyes met, and he began to run toward me. He took me in his arms and his lips met mine. My dreams had only begun.

TWO

A Year to Get Ready

As we drove the ninety miles northeast to our families in Kingsport, all Joe talked about was the island. He had slides, maps, drawings, and ideas.

Sometime during the Christmas holidays, I finally realized—*He's serious about this island!* The questions came like the snow flurries outside the windows: "Do they allow Americans to buy land? Where would you live while you build the house? What about water and electricity? Where do you buy food?"

Our families were equally curious about this outlandish dream, but Joe had an answer for every question. His enthusiasm was contagious, and I was caught in the web of his excitement.

One question went unasked. Did he *really* want me to be a part of all this? Only time would answer that one. Meanwhile, I intended to act as if I were going to Nicaragua with him.

Joe predicted he would need to save ten thousand dollars in the next year in order to buy the island and the building materials and for living expenses during construction. He would also need a truck to get to Nicaragua and a boat for transportation to and from the island.

He decided that he would live in Kingsport with his mother and work as an architect at the firm where he had interned for three summers. I would continue working at TSD and finish school. For a year we would save every penny and sell anything we couldn't use on the island. He assured me everything would work out.

The Christmas break was over too quickly, and I was back in Knoxville going to school and working. But this time was different. I had a purpose, and I was able to see Joe every weekend.

His letters during the week were encouraging. Toward the end of January he wrote, "We can do what we dream, baby, if we just plan and save."

He was always so sure, but I'd never even been out of the United States—much less four thousand miles away from home. After all, he hadn't asked me to marry him yet, and I could never go under any other circumstances. I just kept hoping and praying everything would work as he had said. As the weeks fell behind us, the anticipation rose.

We began to get ready. We sold Joe's beloved Triumph GT-6 to buy a 1966 Chevy truck with a camper for just eleven hundred dollars. The truck had only fifty thousand miles on it and was in perfect condition.

We found a boat and motor at a garage sale. The truck may have been in perfect condition, but the boat was a mess. It looked as if it had been finger-painted in the dark by a class of preschoolers. We spent weeks stripping off black, green, and purple splotches and repainting. I recovered the seats and rewired the lights while Joe fixed the motor.

When she was finally ready for launching, we hitched her behind our light blue pickup. Her royal blue hull was gleaming. What a pair! Since these two vehicles were going to transport us and all we owned to our "promised land," we christened them "Moses" and "Aaron."

We drove to Patrick Henry Lake for a test run. On that chilly April day, we were warmed with the excitement of knowing two major items on our dream list could be marked *done*.

June 5, 1975, finally arrived. I had my degree at last. A flurry of activities ended the school year at TSD, and I said good-by to Knoxville and moved home to Kingsport.

That summer Joe decided we could earn extra money by refinishing his boss's motor yacht. We both worked hard sanding, stripping, staining, and varnishing. One August morning Joe phoned and said, "Can you be ready to go somewhere fancy at around six o'clock?"

"Are you kidding?" I answered incredulously. "Of course, but are you sure we can afford a splurge?"

"Yeah, I've got a surprise—see you later."

I hung up the phone and looked forward to a night out at a nice restaurant. When Joe picked me up he showed me the check for the work on the yacht.

"So that's the surprise!" I cheered. "Where are we going?"

He grinned and said, "You'll see."

Even a drizzling East Tennessee rain couldn't dampen my spirit of celebration.

As we drove out of town, my curiosity got the best of me. "Joe, there aren't any restaurants out here in the boondocks. Where are you taking me?"

"It's not much farther, now," he answered quietly.

We turned onto a one-lane gravel road leading deep into some woods. "Where are we going?" I demanded.

"I missed a turn. I'll have to keep going until I can find a place to turn around."

"There isn't anywhere in here to turn," I said impatiently.

Suddenly, he stopped the truck and announced, "Here we are."

I looked out through the glistening raindrops, and there across a wooden bridge was a picnic shelter with—no, it couldn't be! I couldn't trust my eyes. Underneath the primitive shelter was a table set formally for two.

Joe opened the door of the truck and held out his hand. "May I show you to your table, señorita?"

I looked into his sea-green eyes and still don't remember that my feet ever touched the ground.

Before me was the loveliest table setting I'd ever seen—candles, crystal, china, silver and flowers spread on a linen tablecloth. Everything was perfect. He held my chair and then ran to the back of the truck.

My heart pounded with joy as I watched this beautiful, sensitive man balance a silver tray on his fingertips. He was quickly by my side. "Dinner is served," he intoned as he placed Colonel Sanders' best before me— Kentucky fried chicken, creamed potatoes, and slaw!

I giggled through my tears. For the first time since I'd met Joe, I could think of nothing to say.

When we had finished the chocolate parfait Joe reached for my hand. "Sandy, I've got something to ask you."

He came around the table and knelt on one knee. "I told you a long time ago I'd have to know for certain before I asked someone to be my wife. For nine months you've worked with me toward a dream. Now I can't imagine my life without you, and I want this dream to be *our* dream. Will you marry me?"

A thousand Fourth of Julys exploded inside me. There was no doubt in my mind as I pulled Joe into my arms. Through tears of joy I whispered, "Forever and always I'm yours."

We set the date for December 27, 1975. We'd have a church ceremony and leave for Nicaragua after the reception. Now we had even more plans to make than before.

I started designing and making my wedding dress. We also designed our own wedding rings and had them made by a local goldsmith. A whole new set of lists kept me running from morning until night.

We mailed our wedding invitations in November, and the phone started ringing two days later. What did a couple who was leaving the country to live on an island want for a wedding gift? We happily consulted our lists.

Then the gifts began to arrive: a case of oil, a Coleman stove, floatable flashlights, a first-aid kit, life jackets, a block and tackle. Of course, we needed dishes, towels, and cookware. Each day was filled with unwrapping and sorting, then checking the items off the lists. And the lists grew shorter and shorter.

"How will we get all this stuff in the camper?" I asked when Joe came by after work. He got a gleam in his eye and shouted, "Come on, I've got an idea!"

We drove downtown and pulled into the parking lot of a funeral home. *What now?* I thought as I waited.

A door opened, and Joe and another man carried a huge wooden crate to the back of the truck. "They're giving us two casket shipping crates so you can start packing," he exclaimed triumphantly.

I laughed aloud. "I can imagine our trying to explain these to five sets of border guards."

On the drive back to my house, I began to comprehend the indomitable spirit of my future husband. "You can figure out a solution for every problem can't you?"

The holidays were hectic. So much was happening at once. The big day was approaching quickly! And somehow we'd earned and saved ten thousand dollars and gathered the necessary equipment.

Under the Christmas tree was a big package from Joe's brothers and their wives. We opened it and found a K-Mart eight- by ten-foot tent.

"To think you bought us our first home!" I exclaimed. "Now we've got everything."

"Not quite." Joe ran to the garage.

"What's going on?" I asked, looking around at a roomful of sheepish grins.

Then Joe rolled in a 1902 New Companion treadle sewing machine.

"I can't believe it!" I shouted. He had sensed how much I would like to be able to sew on the island.

Just as I smiled and reached out to hug him, my face clouded over. "But how will we haul it? There's no space for it."

"We'll set it in the boat." And that's where it went.

Christmas day was over too soon, and I fell into bed unable to sleep. I still had books to pack, thank-you notes to write, and wedding decorations to arrange. Everything was caving in on me. When I woke the next morning I felt as if I'd slept on a rock. It finally hit me: *Sandy—you're leaving! You're going to marry this man and follow him to an unknown country!*

I lay there staring at the comfortable room I'd grown up in, looking at the familiar things that had made it my home, and I felt a quiver of doubt.

What am I doing? Will our love be enough?

I wish I could say my heart cried *Yes*, but to be honest, I wanted to run and hide and pretend it *was* all a dream. *There must be something we've forgotten. We can't just leave. What about Mom and Dad, my younger brothers, my grandma—will I ever see them again?*

I'd been so busy with my own plans, I had hardly noticed my family. Now that I was leaving, a horrible wave of regret swept over me and I began to cry.

I wanted to call Joe and plead, "Can't we get an apartment and settle down here in Kingsport?" Only my pride kept me from dialing his number.

Lying there in self-pity, I looked back over the past year. Everything had worked out perfectly—just as Joe had said it would.

"Why is it so hard for me to trust you, God?" I sobbed. "Why am I so sad? I should be the happiest woman in the world."

I heard no answer but I began to see in my mind's eye the swaying palm trees and the smiling faces of people I would meet. I remembered Joe's excitement as he described the island and the simple Nicaraguans who lived nearby. This was my dream, too!

Determined, I sat up, got out of bed, and rushed to my dressing room. Even if I had to fake it for a while, I was going to follow the plan until the spirit of adventure had returned.

I hurried around the house helping my mom cook for the reception, packing things, and going back and forth to the church with decorations. But my frustration was beginning to mount. I thought I'd had all I could take. Then my college roommate pulled into the driveway.

At the sight of her, I burst into tears. My good friend, Cindy! She was bewildered, but she let me use her as a sounding board for my mixed-up emotions. And by evening she had me laughing and reminiscing about my early courtship with Joe.

Joe called that night after the wedding rehearsal. "Sandy, let's borrow my mom's car and go to Gatlinburg for a couple of nights after the wedding so we can relax and rest up from the packing."

"Oh, yes!" I cried with relief. Now I had two extra days in familiar places.

We said good night for the last time as two single people. The next day Joe and I would be husband and wife.

I lay awake—too keyed up to sleep. The minutes ticked away. December 27 was dawning whether I was ready or not.

My Dad called me for breakfast, but I was too nervous to eat. It seemed only moments later that Cindy was helping me into my wedding dress.

"Bob, Earl, Don, are you guys ready?" Mom and Dad were rushing my brothers. "Brush your teeth. Straighten your tie. Comb your hair." Tears welled up in my eyes. I would miss their growing years.

Finally we all piled into the car and drove off to the late-morning ceremony. Bob and Earl giggled. Don was silent. Cindy and I were trying to keep from crying again.

It was time.

All the wedding plans were rushing through my head as I took my place at the back of the church. Had the blue spruce arrived? Had the candles been put on its branches?

Then I saw Joe! He was so handsome, so beautiful. I looked into his eyes and began the slow march up the aisle. Those few steps were taking me into the biggest adventure of my life!

With our parents beside us, we made the vows we had carefully memorized and exchanged our special rings. Then Joe took my arm, and we faced our friends as the minister announced, "I present to you Mr. and Mrs. Joe Barker."

The reception was more like a family reunion. Joe and I wouldn't see our friends or family for a long time. We were happy to see everyone, but it was painful to be saying good-by.

It was snowing as we parked at a beautiful creekside motel. Joe built a fire in the rustic fireplace, and I gazed into the golden flames, tension draining from my body. All the packing and the long miles ahead disappeared from my mind. When Joe took me into his arms, I knew I was where I belonged at last.

Two mornings later, back in Kingsport, I stood at the back of our truck staring at all we owned. It had taken us sixteen hours to pack it all into that six- by eight-foot space.

Joe took pictures of our caravan as my brothers taped *Just Married* signs in the camper windows and made plans for a trip to see us.

Mom, Dad, and Grandma stood in the garage with slumped shoulders and trembling chins. We hugged and cried our last good-bys.

"We need to go now," Joe said. He helped me into the truck. Dad was waving. Mom and Grandma stood beside him with tears running down their cheeks. As Joe put old Moses into reverse and backed out of the driveway, I hung my bride's bouquet on the sun visor.

I trembled all over as I spoke: "Will I ever see them again?"

"We'll be back," Joe said to reassure me. "I know it's hard for you, but you'll never regret it."

I began to cry again. "Please, God, take care of us. . . . Take care of them."

At the end of the street, Joe stopped the truck and reached for my hand. "God," he began, "we're on our way and we need You. Guide us and help us to stay close and take care of those we love. In Jesus' Name, amen."

We drove downtown for the last time. *Strange, how you live somewhere twenty-three years and never see it until you're leaving,* I thought.

Joe began to blow the horn. People in other cars stared at us. I waved excitedly at people I didn't even know, looking into their startled eyes.

"With God's help we're going to make our dreams come true," I said determinedly.

We were on our way to Nicaragua at last.

THREE

On the Road

We drove south on Interstate 75. We were really on our way. "Good-by Tennessee," I said as we drove into Georgia. Joe squeezed my hand. "I love you, Sandy."

With just sixteen more miles to Alabama, I thought of the foreign borders that lay ahead. "Joe, what will going through the borders be like?"

"Don't worry," he said. "If we're friendly and cooperative, they are."

"But, Joe, if they make us unload all this stuff, I don't know what I'll do."

"Look, honey, we'll just have to cross that bridge when we get to it."

I couldn't help worrying.

We arrived in Tuscaloosa late that night. It was too cold to camp, so we found a reasonably priced motel and enjoyed a good night's rest.

The next morning we met Mr. John Walker of the Phifer Wire Company which was donating twenty boxes of screen wire for the roof of our island house. I only hoped Joe's carefully detailed plans would really show the advantages of lightweight roofing. We said good-by and were on the road again.

Just outside town, we changed back into our jeans and checked all six tires. Even with the sewing machine and screen wire, Aaron's wheels were turning smoothly. It was December 31, 1975, the end of a year. I wondered what lay ahead.

We continued south on Interstate 59 toward New Orleans where we would get our visa stamps for the five countries beyond the Mexican border.

21

Fifteen miles from New Orleans we started noticing an increase in traffic. "What's going on?" I wondered aloud.

We crept along, with cars and buses all around us. Joe rolled down the window and got the attention of someone in the nearest car.

"Why is there so much traffic?" he asked.

The guy in that car nearly dropped his teeth. "You mean you don't know?"

Joe just smiled and with his finest Tennessee drawl admitted, "Nope, shore don't."

The people in the car started laughing while we waited for an answer. "It's the Sugar Bowl!" they chorused.

We looked at each other and burst out laughing. We'd been so busy planning our trip we hadn't noticed anything else for months. "It's a good thing we're already leaving the country," Joe said. "They'd throw us out for this!"

Then it dawned on me. We'd made no reservations. "How will we ever find a place to stay?" I asked.

"Don't worry, we'll find a place," Joe answered, always the optimist.

"How?" I whined. "If we do, it'll cost a fortune."

I didn't want to sleep in the back of our truck. Just the thought of the cramped space behind us made me cringe. Besides, it was too cold, and I wanted to look decent for sightseeing and consulate personnel.

We drove on and on. Each hotel sign flashed "No Vacancy."

"What are we going to do?" I moaned.

Suddenly, Joe pulled into a motel parking lot. "Wait here and I'll see what I can do." The red neon sign in front of the truck hammered out, "NO, NO, NO."

Joe was inside at the registration desk. He was waving his arm toward me and talking a mile a minute. The desk clerk smiled and nodded as she placed a key on the counter.

Joe came running out as if he'd just won the Sugar Bowl himself. He climbed into the truck, dangling the key in front of him.

"A truck driver just checked out. The motel maid has already gone home, so we'll have to make our bed, but I didn't think you'd mind that," he exclaimed breathlessly.

"Of course not," I said laughing, "but why did you pull into this particular motel?"

"I don't know. Something just told me to try here."

The next two days we spent sightseeing and visiting the Mexican consulate and a local marina. Joe drooled over every yacht.

"Sure you wouldn't like to buy your dream boat now?" I asked as we walked along the docks.

"No," he answered, "first the island, then the sailboat."

Mexico's consulate was the only one open until Monday. When they assured us we could get our other four visas in Mexico City, we decided to go on.

Interstate 10 stretched west toward Houston where another part of our island house awaited us. Joe had sent the specifications for the steel joints to hold up our roof beams.

Thinking of the perspective he had drawn of the island with the house set proudly among the graceful palms, I said, "I can't wait to see the island."

He glanced at the odometer. "Well, we're one-third there!"

After picking up the steel, we went by the Astrodome and then on to the Corpus Christi marinas. We arrived late that night. It was pouring rain when we began looking for a motel. Joe checked a few but came out shaking his head. "Too much," he told me. "We'll find another one."

Soon we were downtown where our chances of doing that were slim. Joe pulled up to a hotel on the bay and ran in. The place looked expensive. The windshield wipers squeaked as I waited. In a few minutes I saw him leaping over puddles back toward the truck.

"This is it!" he said as he drove around the building to park. I was too tired to care how much it cost.

We unpacked our overnight bags and stood quietly in the elevator. When we got to the room Joe opened the door and swept me off my feet into his arms.

"Joe," I said, sleepy-eyed, "you don't have to. . . ." I stared in amazement as he carried me into the room. This wasn't a room at all—it was a living room, dining room, bedroom and kitchen! "Welcome to the honeymoon suite for just eighteen dollars," he said proudly. "The woman downstairs said this is the off season and she wanted us to have it when she saw the signs in our truck."

When we looked off the balcony the next morning, we could see the bay through the mist. After breakfast, we headed for the docks. There were beautiful yachts moored everywhere.

"No wonder you love sailing so much," I commented as we walked around.

We went into a sailing gear shop and bought some foul-weather gear. Then we bought groceries for our plywood kitchen. This would be our last day in the United States.

We drove south on Highway 77 toward the border. We stopped to wash clothes at Harlingen. In only twenty-four miles I would be in another country.

But it was late. "Let's wait until morning," Joe decided. "It's not a good idea to drive after dark in Mexico."

I sighed with relief. We pulled into the next motel, got a room, and fell into bed exhausted.

FOUR

Traveling with Sanborn

The next morning, after buying travel insurance in Brownsville, we drove up to the United States customs building. At the bridge toll house, we paid our fifty-cent toll for the truck and boat. Then we bore to the left and up and over the Rio Grande.

"No man's land," Joe said.

People were everywhere. He was smiling and waving to everyone. I could hardly speak because there was so much to see. I felt as if I'd stepped across some kind of time line. There were barefoot, half-clothed kids on the muddy river banks. Women with aprons carried food in bowls on their heads. Groups of men were walking along, slapping one another on the back and laughing.

Bienvenidos a sign said as we entered the border town of Matamoros. We stopped and told a uniformed man we were going through to Guatemala. He directed us to the Mexican customs building. Joe went inside to the Immigration Department with our passports. We had our tourist cards validated there and then stopped at my worst dread—*Aduana* (customs) to get our truck and boat permits.

One of the customs officers came out, opened our camper, looked in, and asked, "Where are you going?"

"Nicaragua," Joe answered pointing toward our signs in the windows. "It's our honeymoon, our *luna de miel.*"

The customs officer closed the truck and patted Joe on the back. As he placed a sticker in the front window, he flicked my bouquet hanging on the visor. He winked at me and walked away waving and saying, "*Buen viaje.*"

"That's it?" I exclaimed.

"I told you not to worry, honey," Joe said, and we drove down a beautiful divided boulevard. Children ran up to the truck to sell us fruit and souvenirs. Some just stuck out their palms and shouted, *"Un peso, por favor?"*

I'd never seen so many people in the streets at home except during parades. "Will children come up to us like this everywhere?" I shouted above the noise.

"Well, they're certainly not shy." Joe waved and smiled as we drove along. Our first border now lay behind us.

Soon we were through Matamoros going south on Highway 101. The Sanborn Insurance Agency in Brownsville had provided us with a travelog that told us what to expect every kilometer of the way. As we passed through many communities, I learned: *Paso del Aguila* was Eagle Pass; *El Tejon*, the Badger.

We stopped twice for visa checks and continued a hundred miles to the junction with Highway 180 to Soto la Marina, a village near the sea. It was getting late when we got there and we decided to camp for the night.

We parked first at a café. I couldn't wait to get to the bathroom. My first fluent sentence was whispered shyly, *"Dónde está el baño?"*

The young woman motioned to a curtained-off portion of the room. I stared at it, looked around at all the people eating, and went back to the table where Joe had sat down.

"What am I going to do?" I whispered to Joe.

"That depends on how badly you need to go," he answered with an impish grin. I glanced around the room. I either had to forget modesty and live or sit there and die. I jumped up, walked across the room to the curtain, and went in. My feet stuck out underneath, and I thought I'd never be able to go. People were talking and laughing, but I just knew they'd all get quiet the minute I made a sound. They didn't.

When I had returned to the table, Joe asked loudly, "Did everything come out all right?" I thought I'd die right there until I suddenly realized none of these people could understand him.

He congratulated me as if I'd just received my diploma. "You're learning, woman."

We ordered some food. It wasn't Taco Bell, but it was good, and the grape soda was tasty, too. It was getting dark outside by that time and I knew Joe didn't want to drive any farther until morning.

"Where are we going to stay?" I asked. There were no KOA campgrounds around. Joe walked over to the woman who had served us. He was gesturing as much as talking. He walked the woman to the screen door and pointed toward our truck. She grinned and said, *"Sí."* She wiped her wrinkled hands on her apron, then gestured to the side of the café.

Turning toward me she made a motion that I thought meant go away. I stared at her in confusion.

"Come on," Joe said, "that's their sign to come." So much to learn.

Next thing I knew, Joe was pulling the truck into somebody's backyard alongside a chicken house and a pig pen.

"Aren't these people just incredible?" he asked me. I stared at him with my eyebrows up, a forced grin on my face. "She wants us to stay here in their yard tonight!"

I tried to keep smiling. The woman was stroking my blond hair and saying "Okay, Okay," over and over. Hoping she would not sense my apprehension, I hugged her.

Joe helped me get the suitcase out of the truck. I got a towel and washcloth and headed for the café. "Want me to go along?" he asked.

"Please," I whimpered as I side-stepped manure.

I felt better knowing Joe would guard the curtain while I washed off. My face was caked with dust, and the water felt good and cool. Just seven days earlier I'd been soaking in a big bubble bath at a hotel in Tuscaloosa, Alabama. *Our first night out of the USA and I'm already homesick,* I thought as I dried my face.

We walked back to the truck in silence. I squeezed through the piles of equipment and stretched out on the camper bed. I lay awake for a long time just listening to the animal sounds outside the window. "I want to go back," I almost said, just as Joe turned toward me and began, "God, thank You for being with us today. Help us to stay close, and give us patience. Thank You for these kind people who have welcomed us into their home. Be with us tomorrow as we travel toward Mexico City and. . . ." I turned over and looked out the window. Countless stars twinkled in the velvety sky. "Help me!" I prayed silently before I fell asleep.

A rooster's crow woke me up. *Where am I,* I thought as I stared into darkness. Remembering, I found Joe's watch on the curtain rod. Two-thirty!

Morning finally came. As we got ready to leave, the woman came out

to check on us and offer us breakfast. When Joe tried to pay her for allowing us to sleep in her yard, she shook her head, so he dug around in the
camper for a few minutes and placed a scented candle and holder in her
hands. "Please, then, take this gift as a token of our gratitude." She
smiled and bowed her head, shyly admiring the gift.

So this is why he loves these people so much, I thought, realizing she had
befriended us with no thought of payment. I had a feeling the road ahead
would reveal a Mexico I had heard little of.

We left the tiny village for Tampico to get on the ferry crossing the
Panuco River and go on to Tuxpan. In Tampico we stopped in a heavy
stream of cars. I was burning up. My hair stuck to the back of my neck,
and I was getting more and more disgusted.

The ferry was closed for repairs, so Joe got out our map to search for an
alternate route to Mexico City.

Just then someone walked up to the window of the truck. "Hello!"
said a voice with a British accent. "Are you waiting for the ferry?"

We looked up from the map and nodded. A tall, blond man motioned
toward an older model Cadillac with a camper behind it. Inside were a
dark-haired woman and two small children. He stuck out his hand and
grasped Joe's firmly. "Andy Grayston from Ontario, Canada."

Something about his friendly smile, his wife's calm expression, and
the freckled faces of his two little girls made us feel as if we had just run
into long-lost friends. Their English was comforting, too.

Joe and I got out of the truck. He spread out the map on the hood, and
I walked over to the car.

"Hi!" I said. The little girls giggled. "She talks funny, Mommy."

"Hello, I'm Barbara, and these two are Jenny and Leigh."

I stuck out my hand and introduced myself, "Sandy from Tennessee."

She smiled and said, "I knew you must be from the South with that
accent." She went on to explain that her husband was an electrician and
that they were on vacation. She seemed completely unruffled by the
heat and the delay.

"We're on our way to an island in Nicaragua," I began as Joe and Andy
walked up. "Hey, Babs," Andy said enthusiastically, "you want to try a
different route with these folks?"

Joe shoved the map in the window and pointed out another highway
that went through the mountains. She glanced at it and said, "Sure, why
not?"

I was already frustrated by the change in plans, but this woman with two small children was saying, "Why not?" How could she be so complacent?

I walked back to the truck. Joe and Andy were too busy talking to people in cars all around us for me to demand an explanation. People started moving their cars to let our caravan of truck, boat, and now Cadillac and camper turn around and take the opposite direction.

I sensed Joe's satisfaction, and he sensed my apprehension. "Don't worry, hon, it will be okay," he said, patting my leg. "It'll be an adventure to take a different route."

In the side mirror, I could see Andy, Barbara, and the girls behind us. *If she can do it, I can.* I kept my apprehension inside.

"Don't you feel as if we've known these people a long time?" Joe asked.

"I guess so," I agreed. Then I blurted out, "Where *are* we going?"

Joe pointed to the map. A black line wriggled toward Mexico City. I consulted the legend and commented dryly, "Well, at least it's paved." At a fork in the highway, Joe needed directions so he pulled up alongside a man carrying a huge sack on his back. "¿A Mexico?" he asked.

The man pointed one direction and smiled. "Short cut," he said.

"How about that?" Joe said in amazement. "It's going to be faster, too."

I couldn't share his enthusiasm. If this was a shortcut, why would they have built a ferry?

"I can't believe we're going to follow his directions!" I argued. "He's probably never even been in a car!" As I sat there fuming we were already on our way.

We drove for hours, and finally the sun was sinking in the west. "Now what are we going to do?" I asked. We had passed only three or four houses and acres and acres of farmland.

About a mile ahead, I could see smoke. Joe said, "We'll check up there. That's probably a cooking fire."

He pulled to the side of the road and stopped. Watching him sprint the two hundred yards toward the ranch house, I got out to stretch my legs. The Graystons were getting out of their car. The girls were wide-eyed and hungry.

"We'll eat soon," Barbara told them confidently.

Joe was talking to a dark-skinned woman. Her black hair was pulled back, and she was barefoot. Several naked children were hiding behind her.

"Is Joe getting directions?" Andy asked.

"I don't know," I replied. "He's probably talking them into letting us stay here."

Joe was gesturing and smiling. The woman craned her neck to look our way. She smiled and nodded her head.

The sun had just dropped out of sight when he came running back to us. "They want us to stay here," he panted.

"Wonderful!" Andy exclaimed.

So, there we were. We drove the few hundred yards to the back of the ranch house in the dark. Someone carrying a lantern walked toward us. We stopped the truck, and the light came closer. Joe leaned out the window.

"*Hola!*" a man spoke. He was smiling below a straw hat and straight black hair. "Okay," he said, motioning that we were parked just where he wanted us. We thanked him as he waved and walked off.

After a quick supper of sandwiches, we told our new friends good night and crawled into the camper. I lay there staring into the darkness.

"See how great these people are?" Joe whispered.

"I'm seeing one thing—you never meet a stranger," I answered. "How can you be so confident all the time? I wish I didn't worry so much."

Joe hugged me. "Don't let it bug you. One of us needs to be cautious. That's what makes us the perfect team."

"I hope you're right."

The next morning I woke up perspiring. I threw off the sheet and reached for the sliding window. At home in Tennessee we would have been cold, and here in Mexico we were sweating.

I pulled back the curtain and shouted, "Oh, my goodness, Joe, look outside!" He turned over quickly. We stared into the propeller of an airplane.

"Did you see this plane here last night?" I asked. "No!" he exclaimed. "Now I know why this was such a level parking place. We're on the landing strip for a crop duster!"

We quickly put on some clothes and stepped outside. Barbara and Andy were already up and preparing breakfast. I dug out our brand new Coleman stove, reread the directions, and got a flame going.

Barbara walked toward me with a basket. "Look what these lovely people brought out for us," she said, showing me the fresh eggs, bread, and fruit.

"Where are your little girls?" I asked. She pointed toward the ranch house where Jenny and Leigh were playing with the Mexican children under a tree. "No cultural barrier for those two!"

I picked out some eggs and two pieces of bread and started preparing our breakfast. Joe turned from the camper. "Sandy, have you seen the truck keys?"

"Oh, no, don't tell me," I answered. "Surely you didn't lose them in all that mess." After eating, we searched fruitlessly for the missing keys. "We'll just have to use my set and get some new ones made," I commented in disgust. "How could you be so careless?"

My wavering confidence was crumbling.

We gave the family a flashlight as a token of our appreciation and asked directions to Mexico City. They assured us we were on the right road.

We passed three cars during the next eight hours of driving. The map in our Sanborn's travel guide showed six villages on this highway, and we had passed only two. We didn't know exactly where we were or how long it would take to get to *la Capital.*

"Look," Joe exclaimed. I looked up from the map, and in the distance were huge mountains.

"Are we going to have to cross those?" I wondered aloud.

"I don't know since I've never been this way before. But remember Mexico City is seven thousand feet above sea level, so we're going to have to go up sometime."

The mountains jutted up from the plains larger than life. We climbed steeply on a winding two-lane road. It was getting late in the afternoon and we didn't know where we were. The temperature dropped as we climbed higher.

"Old Moses feels like he's back home, doesn't he?" I joked with Joe, trying to ease the tension.

"If this old truck pulls these roads with our heavy load, we'll never need to worry about it again," he answered.

Soon it was dark and we ran into dense fog. Even at home in the hills of Tennessee, we'd never seen it this thick. Every once in a while, seemingly out of nowhere, headlights would glare through the fog as a bus roared past. My neck and shoulders were tight, and I just hoped we would get somewhere soon. We couldn't even pull off the road because there was no visible shoulder.

Andy's headlights blinked at us, signaling car trouble. "What are we going to do now?" I asked. "We can't stop right in the road."

"I'm going to have to stop and see what's wrong," Joe stated matter-of-factly.

His shoulders were hunched with tension, too. He eased the truck to the edge of the pavement and put it in neutral, leaving it running. He jumped out and yelled, "Keep your foot on the brake!" He didn't need to tell me that.

He came back in a few seconds and jumped in. "Andy's car is smoking and steaming like crazy! It could be his water pump. You know what he said to me?"

"What?" I asked, trying to control the fear welling inside me.

"He said we'd just have to trust God to get us to a village soon."

I sat there staring into the cloudy vapors boiling around us. *Who does this guy think he is, anyway?* I thought. Sure, I'd grown up in church and asked God about really important things, but I didn't think He was into providing mechanical assistance in the middle of Mexico. After all, He expected us to take care of ourselves, didn't He?

We drove another mile on the twisting mountain road. Those buses had come from somewhere, but where and how far?

Just as Andy's blinking lights told us he was desperate, Joe shouted, "Look ahead!"

Through the fog we saw the dim glare of a neon sign. The now-familiar *Pemex* sign indicated we had arrived at one of Mexico's state-controlled gasoline stations.

We bumped down a steep drive and stopped at the pumps. Andy pulled in directly behind us, steam pouring out all around the hood of his car.

A young man in a crumpled uniform strolled out. Joe held out his hand and greeted the fellow as if he'd known him all his life. The young man spoke in English, "Hungry?" We nodded. Then, *"Mecánico?"* he added, pointing to Andy's car. Again we nodded. He grinned and said, "Welcome."

In English, Joe asked, "Is there a hotel nearby?"

The young man looked puzzled. "I no speak English," he admitted. He knew those few words and that was it.

Joe began speaking and gesturing.

"He says there's a hotel in the village, and he can get somebody to fix your car, too." It sure was a good thing one of us knew the language.

Under the blanket of fog, it was difficult to see exactly where we were, so we followed another young man on a bicycle.

We walked inside the hotel which was a small café on a street corner and sat down. People began to stare. This was obviously not one of the main tourist towns in Mexico.

We ordered something to eat, and though I didn't know what I was eating, it was warm and filling. Then a man told us he would show us a safe place to park for the night.

We drove through some gates and saw a dozen cars and trucks parked inside a high stucco wall with broken bottles jutting up around the perimeter. These were the only other vehicles we'd seen in this village.

"He says we can now sleep well knowing our things will be guarded all night."

We got out our overnight bag and followed the man to the Hotel Augusto. It was very cold. He told Joe they'd had snow flurries a week earlier. What a shock! One by one my preconceived notions about hot, dusty, bandit-filled Mexico were being dispelled.

The room was dimly lit by a single bulb hanging from the ceiling. The faded walls looked as if they had been painted with a ridged roller. The designs scrawled nervously up and down. To my surprise, there was a bathroom! I was so glad to see the shower. But when I turned the control marked "C," which should have meant *caliente* for hot, there was only cold water. At that moment there was a soft knock at our door.

I stood motionless trying to hear as Joe talked with someone for a few seconds, then closed the door. "The owner said for us to wait til morning if we want hot water."

"It's already been two days since I was clean," I sighed. "One more won't make that much difference."

Sure enough, the next morning there was hot water, and I felt like a new woman when I emerged from the hotel room. Glancing down the hall I saw a young boy not more than eight years old placing sticks of wood under a big steel tank.

"Joe," I called, opening our door, "come here a minute. Ask him what he's doing, will you?"

Joe conversed with him and said, "This is a wood-fueled water heater.

He has been keeping this fire going since 3 A.M. so we would have hot water."

I was so touched I nearly cried. I thought of my own young brothers who have to be forced to mow the yard. Here was this youngster who cheerfully did a job for a bunch of strange-looking visitors. I was definitely falling in love with these friendly people, just as Joe had said I would.

After breakfast I got out a clown puppet I had used at Tennessee School for the Deaf. Children and adults gathered around to watch Bozo's antics. I enjoyed watching the people laugh as much as they enjoyed watching the clown.

Incredibly, Andy's car was repaired in a couple of hours, and we were on our way again.

Joe taught me Spanish as we drove. I felt like a child repeating my numbers and ABC's, but I wanted to communicate with these people for myself.

Since leaving the USA, I had already begun to change. Traveling with Andy and Barbara, finding the village when we needed it, and the smiling face of the little boy all had given me a confidence I'd never before experienced.

That day we saw wonderful sights in and around those beautiful mountains. In the afternoon we finally began to see signs clearly indicating that we were on the right road and would pass the famous Pyramids of Teotihuacan.

A couple of hours before dark, we pulled into the parking lot at the archaeological site and explored the ruins. The Graystons agreed to camp near us for one more night so we could do more exploring the next day.

"We'll be going on to the Pacific coast tomorrow," they told us as we sat around the campfire later. "We're glad we ran into you. And we hope the island plans work out, too."

It had been wonderful getting to know this Canadian family. Despite delays and disappointments Andy had been unwaveringly sure that all would work out for the best. And Barbara demonstrated loyalty and trust in her husband. Both were adventurous enough to go against all advice and travel with their two little girls through unknown country. They had a quality about them Joe and I appreciated.

We said good-by the next morning and drove on to Mexico City. According to our Sanborn's guide, we could camp right downtown. We found Cabello Trailer Park and settled in.

The next morning we were on sleek subways zooming from one end of town to another. "I feel so strange being in such a big city after the tiny villages we've been in," I commented to Joe.

"Just think! This is all a lot of foreigners ever see of Mexico!" he replied.

We went to Zócalo square and the big cathedral. We found several consulate offices, but they were all closed after 2 P.M. We were learning about South-of-the-Border time.

We practically ran from one place to another and still got caught in the rush hour at five o'clock. The clean, uncrowded subway of the morning hours became a suffocating, surging mass of people.

"Now you know why I advised you not to bring your purse," Joe yelled.

The next day we were up early and took a cab directly to the Nicaraguan consulate and then on to El Salvador's. We were able to tour the Museum of Anthropology, visit Chapultepec Park, and shop for groceries before the evening rush.

That evening Joe invited me for one last splurge at the famous House of Tiles restaurant. He studied the menu—written in both English and Spanish. I tried to pronounce some things, and he said, "Don't worry, I'll order tonight. You can practice more."

The waiter came and said, *"Buenos noches."* I returned the greeting and Joe gave him our order. As he spoke, the waiter tried to keep from laughing. I wondered what Joe had said. From the look on his face, he apparently didn't know what was funny either.

Then, in beautiful English, the waiter spoke. "Sir, you have just ordered a broiled tractor!"

I wanted to roll on the floor laughing. "So, *I* need to practice more, huh? Well, the masquerade is over. I'm going to start learning my own Spanish. There's no telling what you've said to people along the way. No wonder you use your hands so much when you talk!"

Joe was laughing, too. "Okay, okay, a little broiled tractor never hurt anyone!"

And so, the pedestal I had placed Joe on since our wedding had another tiny crack. Even though it was a funny mistake, I began to wonder and my confidence waned.

The next morning we drove out of Mexico City on Highway 95 toward Cuautla. We hoped to get to Oaxaca by night. We descended out of the mountains and continued southeast toward Guatemala.

That afternoon we turned west toward the coast and my first view of the Pacific. After finding a secluded spot in a nice campground with a swimming pool, we headed for the ocean.

When we came back for a shower, we discovered the only facilities were outside at the pool. "Everybody down here is like family when it comes to bathrooms," I told Joe as we began to lather up—swimsuits and all. "It's a far cry from the privacy I've grown up with!"

Private or not, it felt good to wash my hair. After supper, we climbed into the camper. "Just one more day in Mexico," Joe said as we snuggled under the sheet.

The next day we drove on and on until we arrived at Camino Real, a nice hotel at Tapachula—last stop in Mexico. After swimming, eating, and taking a shower, we fell exhausted into bed.

The Guatemala border lay just thirteen miles ahead. Our Sanborn travel guide said customs would only be open for four hours the next day. Even though we were up early and got there by 8:30, plenty of cars were already waiting to be checked through.

Finally, it was our turn. Two guards asked to see what we had in the boat. Joe dutifully pulled back the tarp. There was my beautiful treadle machine surrounded by twenty boxes of screen wire. One of the guards picked up a box and said, "*Abralo, por favor.*" Joe opened it and tried to explain why we had all the wire. He finally got out his portfolio and showed them pictures of our proposed house. Their faces just became more puzzled and curious. I tried to be calm and smile a lot, but I was getting more concerned about their attitude.

Then they looked in the camper and began to wrinkle their faces into frowns.

"Unload it," they demanded as if we had only to open a suitcase.

Tears filled my eyes. "I can't do it!" I cried. "I just can't."

Joe began to talk with the guards, and they continued shaking their heads. Other cars were being checked through and pulling around us. Finally Joe came over to me.

"Did you talk them out of it?" I asked expectantly.

"No," he answered with disappointment, "we're going to have to do it."

I slumped down on the steps and started crying like a spoiled child. "I'm three thousand miles from home, I can't talk above a three-year-old level, and I'm tired," I sobbed.

The guards looked down at me with disgust written all over their faces. That made me cry even harder. Someone at a desk motioned for Joe to come to him. After a few minutes Joe sat down beside me.

"There is one way we can do this without unloading," he said help-lessly. "That official over there said we can hire a guard to ride through the country with us, and we'll be in El Salvador by tonight."

"Okay," I said through my tears. "But he can't smoke. It will make me sick."

Joe was smiling again as he walked back to the desk. The man stamped our passports and called for a guard.

We hurriedly loaded the screen while the guards argued over who would have to go with us and not smoke. We were finally going into Guatemala, and I couldn't wait to get out. "I never thought I'd be joined on my honeymoon by a military escort with—a machine gun in his lap," I said to Joe as we pulled out from under the customs carport.

It took us eight hours to drive to the next border. We stopped at several checkpoints. We let the guard out as we pulled away from the last check-point and drove up the steep hillside to the El Salvador customs station. The officials there waved us through without looking at anything but our passports.

"What a difference from one border to the next!" I said.

"Part of the reason is the people on duty," Joe tried to explain, "and of course the political climate has a whole lot to do with it."

We spent the night on the beach at San Diego and drove to Honduras the next morning through beautiful tunnels cut through cliffs dropping into the ocean. We passed winding rivers spilling into the sea.

Another border, Honduras. With hardly a wave, we were on our way again. At a tiny village we bought fresh cantaloupe and ice cream. Never had I tasted melons so sweet nor ice cream so rich.

As we drove on toward the Nicaraguan border, I could hardly contain my excitement. "We're almost there," I shouted out the windows at the sky.

We pulled into a gas station in Honduras and ate at a restaurant next door. As we finished eating, Joe asked the waitress, "Is there anywhere to camp nearby?" I was already going to the back of the truck to get out my makeup bag and towel when he turned around.

"I know," I said, laughing. "They said we're welcome to stay right here, didn't they?"

Joe put his arms around me and pulled me close. "You're catching on, aren't you?" he whispered. "Tomorrow is the big day."

"Donde está el baño?" I asked the woman inside. *"No hay,"* she replied shaking her head. *No bathroom!* I thought in dismay as she motioned to a leaning outdoor johnny. Even though I wanted to look nice the next morning, I was determined not to get discouraged. Rummaging around in my bath supplies, I got an idea.

I returned to the restaurant with our copper kettle and asked for some water. After the woman filled it for me, I crawled back into the camper. We had brought a Sears "port-a-potty," and I figured I was going to have a shower one way or another.

I filled my douche bag with water and hung it on a clothes hook. Sitting on the potty, I let the water flow as I needed it and was able to take a shower.

Joe heard the water and cracked open the camper door. "Hey, what's going on in there?" He surveyed my rig, and he started laughing as he closed the door.

I felt wonderful as I crawled into the bed. As I got comfortable, Joe climbed in with another kettle of water. "If you can do it, so can I!"

Awhile later he was lying beside me. "You're doing great, Sandy," he said, kissing the back of my head. "Tomorrow night we should be at Puerto Asese where we'll put the boat in the water. Our dream is coming true."

FIVE

Nicaragua—at Last

The next morning we were on the road at dawn. "We'll make a phone call if we have to," Joe assured me as we approached the sign announcing the *frontera*.

"Do you think that will be necessary?" I asked. I was so happy to be arriving at our new home that I had no anxiety about the final border.

The men stared at us and asked what our signs said. I had learned enough Spanish to answer, "It is our honeymoon, and this crazy gringo has driven me four thousand miles to meet you and see your beautiful country."

Their faces lit up with pride, and they patted Joe on the back. One of the guards took my arm and introduced me to all the people selling souvenirs and exchanging money along the station sidewalk. Joe walked from one of the offices waving our passports. "Let's go, *amor*; we are in!" I loved being called sweetheart in Spanish.

We hopped into the truck and shouted, "*Mucho gusto*," to all our newfound friends. "*Buen viaje*," they shouted back, whistling and waving.

A couple of hours later we were driving around the sharp curves of the hill descending into the city of Managua. In his excitement Joe was driving fast. "We're finally here!" he shouted.

"Slow down!" I moaned, tightening my seat belt. He acted as if I hadn't said a word, and the boat swayed behind us.

"Over there is the refinery. Up ahead is a new shopping center. To your right is the concrete plant." He talked as fast as he was driving. I could hardly look at anything other than the road. I pressed my foot into the floor, wishing I could brake at every turn.

"I've waited so long to share it all with you. I love it here."

We wove in and out of traffic. "We'll go straight to the dock tonight," Joe said as we bumped along. The street was made of a funny-shaped tile. "They replaced the pavement with these special concrete tiles that can be repaired more easily," Joe explained. "See that broken rubble over there? That used to be wall-to-wall buildings."

On some of the lots were crude cardboard houses where people actually lived. On others were wooden clapboard houses, brightly painted and fenced off with flowers. We stopped at a traffic light, and I stared ahead at an old homemade wagon pulled by oxen. Behind us was a chauffeur-driven Mercedes-Benz. "Talk about extremes," I commented.

"This is what I wrote to you about. Isn't it an incredible country?"

I wondered what the man in the ox cart thought. Did he think it incredible? Joe interrupted my thoughts as we sped along the streets through what was once this nation's thriving capital city.

We entered an older section of town. Houses sprawled out the full width of the lots behind beautifully landscaped, walled entrances. The few windows on the street were covered with wrought iron bars or intricate grill work.

As we continued south out of Managua, I was surprised to see an attractive shopping center much like those at home in the United States.

"Lots of people rebuilt out here in the suburbs after the earthquake," Joe explained.

Suddenly my attention was drawn to a familiar sign on the right. "McDonald's! Now I do feel at home."

Since leaving Mexico City, we had only been through small villages. Managua's shopping centers, four-lane highways, and sprawling suburbs made me feel we had finally returned to the twentieth century.

We bumped along the highway. Signs indicated how many kilometers to Granada—only forty more. "That means just a few miles from the eighteenth century for me!" I joked, wondering what island life would really be like.

Outside Managua's city limits, the road narrowed to two lanes once more. The Pan-Am Highway stretched toward our new home.

"Look up ahead," Joe said as we came around a sharp curve.

On either side of the highway were acres of black porous rock. To my right a smoking mountain rose hundreds of feet above the rocky plain. "What is this?"

"Volcan Santiago! I'll take you up there sometime. You can see right down into the fiery center."

"My brothers will definitely want to see this." Feeling a twinge of homesickness, I wanted to share all these new experiences with our families.

Up ahead to my left was another huge hill. "That looks like a castle up there," I said.

"That's an old Spanish fort," Joe began. "Gosh, there's so much to show you!"

We came to a crowded intersection. "This is the entrance to Masaya—the crafts center I told you about."

My mind was racing with questions, amazement, and excitement. I just couldn't take it all in. Only a few more miles to Granada.

I saw stucco walls and tile roofs ahead. There was a beautiful building to our left. The green carpet of grass surrounding it looked like a golf course. *"El Club Jockey,"* the sign said. Even I could understand that Spanish.

We continued down the narrow streets to the downtown area. Tall, elegant palms swayed gently above the crowded park below, and glaring, white-columned buildings loomed on either side of the street.

Joe turned left onto a long divided boulevard. About a mile ahead I could see the dark green water stretching for miles out to the horizon.

"It does look like the ocean!" I exclaimed. Whitecaps appeared out on the water as the wind tossed the waves along the dark brown shoreline.

Joe reached over and pulled me close to him. "Sandy, only two more miles and the dream really begins. I'm the happiest man alive! I love you!"

Tears filled my eyes and spilled down my cheeks. "I love you, too," I said.

We drove along the shore and turned back inland. "We have to go to the other side of the peninsula to get to the dock," Joe said.

I looked at our mileage. We had driven 3,867 miles without even a flat tire!

I held tightly to Joe's hand and lowered my head. "Thank You, Lord, for bringing us so far. Please continue to lead us. In Jesus' Name."

We turned left and the pavement ended. Tall trees and thick underbrush shaded the narrow gravel road. Up ahead was an open gate.

I gasped as we drove through. There were a refreshment stand and a thatched roof shelter beneath a spreading shade tree. A little monkey scampered down and began to screech wildly. Stone walls without mortar divided the parking area from the boat ramp. Side by side, boats of all shapes and sizes were bobbing up and down in the dark green water. Beyond the boats, dozens of emerald islands dotted the shimmering water. Their towering coconut trees seemed to beckon me. "Oh, Joe," I cried, "it's beautiful! I can't wait to see our island."

"I know you've waited a long time, but you'll have to wait one more night," Joe said. "It'll be dark soon, and we have to get the boat ready for launching before we can see anything."

We were so close and yet so far away. I thought I'd never get to sleep. Our brand new tent lay in its box beneath us. Would we be sleeping in it the next night? How long would the Coleman stove fuel last? What would the islanders think of me?

I peered out the camper window at the flickering fireflies over the water. Each yellow glow brought another question to my mind. *Tomorrow—will you ever come?*

SIX

The Islands

Joe's watch said 4:30 A.M. I heard voices near the truck. I opened the curtain a little and saw about a dozen dugouts gliding toward a dirt ramp along the shore. Men and women carrying huge baskets and empty sacks stepped out. A bus rumbled up and they all got in.

"Where are they going so early?" I asked Joe. He was still asleep and answered with a grunt as the bus pulled away.

Joe turned over and sighed, "They're going to the market." *To market?*, I thought. *Wow, do they get an early start around here! Come to think of it, what am I doing so wide awake at this time of the morning? Of course! Today I'm going to our island!*

"Joe, wake up," I whispered urgently. "We've got to unload the boat and get the motor out from under us. I can't wait any longer!"

Joe popped up like a jack-in-the-box, bumping his head on the top of the camper. Next thing, he was bearding my neck with his two-day stubble, and I began screaming, "You rascal, you've been faking it! How can you lie here when there're islands to be explored?"

He was squirming into his shorts and teasing me, "Okay, lady, last one out has to dump the potty!"

I grabbed for my shorts and top and started wiggling into them as fast as I could. I couldn't even imagine standing up to dress any more. In fourteen days we had learned to make do with our cramped accommodations.

The thing I'd missed most since leaving the USA was clean, available, public restrooms. Not even here at this nice dock was there running water or a bathroom.

As I reached for my hairbrush I shuddered at the thought of what I must look like. From a dressing room of my own to a rearview mirror! I thought, *Lord, You sure are going to have to do a work in my life to get me used to this.*

"You coming or not?" Joe called. He was already taking the tarp off the boat. I stepped down from the camper and straightened up. Imagining the worst about my appearance, I asked hesitantly, "You still like me?"

Joe was pulling boxes of screen wire out of the boat and looked up. "Do I like you?" he said incredulously. "Have you noticed the bum you run around with lately? Come on and help me. We'll both feel better when we can clean up."

Well, no time to worry about my looks. I began to unload clothes and camping supplies in order to get to the motor in the camper. Finally, at about 8 A.M. we were ready to put Aaron in the water.

"Are you sure you know the way to the island?" Then I noticed the huge black rocks in the water around the dock. "All we'd need is to hit a rock with the motor and we'd really be in a fix."

Joe didn't hear me. He was unhooking the straps that held Aaron to the trailer. "This is it!"

I forgot my worries for the moment and watched as Joe backed the boat down the gravel ramp. "Whoa!" I shouted as the boat began to float.

"Hold the brake!" Joe yelled as he cut off the engine. I ran around the truck and jumped in as he jumped out. I could just imagine all our stuff going into the lake if the truck began to roll. In a few seconds Joe shouted again, "Pull it on up and park it."

I parked and locked the truck and camper.

"Hurry!" Joe shouted impatiently. Elephants were trampling in my stomach.

As I stooped over to jump in, Joe reached up and caught me around the waist and took me into his arms. The boat rocked gently as he set me down. "Sandy, welcome to our Nicaragua." As his mouth met mine we heard a whistle from the refreshment stand. The young fellow called out something to us and clapped. Joe was embarrassed and let go of me. He murmured back, "Okay, okay."

He primed the engine and pushed the starter. It cranked immediately. We looked at each other with surprise. After all the miles! With no more ado, we were speeding across the waves into the bay at the foot of the towering inactive volcano—Mombacho.

We sped past island after island. My eyes filled with tears of joy. All I could say over and over was, "A real live Disney World."

Joe's hair streamed back as we skimmed along. His face was full of contentment. He pointed out different islands where he had met people fifteen months earlier. About two miles from the dock we neared a beautiful island with a nice house, dock, and motor boat. "That's where the Americans I told you about live."

I was anxious to meet this retired couple—the Wilsons. But that could wait. Now we were on our way to *our* island.

We veered left toward an opening that led around the peninsula. Only a few islands lay between us and the open lake. Beyond our island one hundred miles of water separated us from Costa Rica. We went around one last island in the middle of the channel.

"There it is!" Joe cried out.

Suddenly the wind became much stronger. Waves threatened to capsize the boat. Our joy turned to frustration as we realized there was no way to proceed safely. I stared ahead. Only one-half mile from us lay our sparkling jewel, and we had no way to get to it!

"Oh, Joe, what are we going to do?" The wind tore the words from my mouth.

Joe was so frustrated he could hardly speak. I caught the words "Go . . . Wilsons' . . . Mercedes."

Within a few minutes, we were back in calmer water and returning to the Americans' island.

"I can't believe it!" Joe shouted above the roar of our engine. "I don't remember it's being so rough."

"How many times were you out here?" I questioned accusingly. "How do you know it isn't like this most of the time?" Though Joe didn't answer, his eyes flashed and his grin turned downward. I immediately felt terrible. *Why can't I keep my big mouth shut?* I thought.

I saw the Wilsons' island to the left. The frame house perched beneath gigantic mango trees. We pulled alongside the rock and concrete and stepped onto the dock.

A trim, gray-haired man bounded down the paved walkway toward us.

His eyes were twinkling as he spoke. "Welcome! So you finally made it!"

From the house came another voice. "Len, send them up. I know they're thirsty. You kids want some Kool-Aid?" A raspy cough followed.

"That's the Mrs.," Mr. Wilson chuckled. "You'd better hurry on up there. She's really glad to have company."

"I'm Sandy," I said, patting his arm. "It's good to meet you." I made my way up the walkway and through the screened-in porch.

"Mrs. Wilson?" I peered into the comfortable one-room house. Twin beds faced me as I pulled the screen door behind me. I almost gasped at the woman before me. Her short-cropped white hair was stained bright red in places from Merthiolate. Her thin sheath of skin seemed translucent over her bones. Every breath was a struggle as she shuffled slowly from the refrigerator.

"It's Bea and Len," she demanded with a snort. "As you can see I'm in poor shape, but it's a good sight better than Los Angeles." She paused to breathe. "Len and I came down here four years ago for my health. You name it, I've got it—diabetes, emphysema, and all the complications that go with them. At least the air is clean here and I'm left alone."

She motioned for me to sit down in one of the rockers facing the beds. I tried not to stare as she handed me a glass of Kool-Aid. "Oh, don't take me wrong." She paused to suck in a breath. "I'm glad for your company. It's nice to speak English to somebody for a change. Well, tell me, how do you like it so far?"

She slumped down on her pillow and stretched out waiting for me to speak. I couldn't get my mouth to work. I'd never seen anyone in such poor physical condition except in a hospital.

When I didn't say anything she chuckled in her raspy way and said, "It's great to get away from the States, isn't it? We got so tired of pollution, dirty politics, and unemployment, we were glad to get here." Again, a gasp for air.

Oh, no, I thought, *she thinks Joe and I are here to get away from something. How can I ever explain to her that this is a dream made possible by the fact that we were born in a land of opportunity?* I started to speak when the door opened and Len and Joe walked in. Joe thanked her for the cold drink and sat down in the other rocker.

There was a wheelchair at the foot of the other bed, and Len sat down in it. "This is what I brought her here in," he said patting the arm. "Yep, she's a sight better than when we first arrived."

Suddenly Bea leaned over on the bed and loudly passed some gas. I know my eyes must have been as big as saucers, but Joe and I both acted as if we hadn't heard a thing since neither Len nor Bea acted like anything was out of the ordinary. They just continued griping.

Bea's rhythmic struggle for breath rattled on as we learned more about this unique couple. Len explained that he couldn't work with any more smart alecks in the U.S. and that he had sold everything to move to Nicaragua.

"Who wants to live in that godforsaken place, anyway?" he asked not really wanting a reply. "Food was sky high, the air was filthy, taxes ate up what we made. . . ." I listened in shock as he went on and on.

Finally they asked how things were going with us. Joe explained the problem we'd had, and Mr. Wilson snickered with a cunning gleam in his eye.

"Do you know which island I'm talking about?" Joe asked.

"Why, no, of course not," Mr. Wilson replied matter-of-factly. "I never venture off the course from my island to the dock."

"You mean you never visit any other islands?" I asked in disbelief.

"Nope," he said, shaking his head. "Too dangerous. Might tear the bottom out of my boat on a rock. Besides gas is too high to cruise around for no reason."

I was astounded. These people lived in one of the most beautiful places I'd ever seen and couldn't even enjoy it. The back of my neck was getting stiff with tension.

"We'd better be going," Joe said finally. "We've got a lot to do." I was relieved.

Len walked us down to the dock. "Now, Joe—I'll expect you to borrow some of my tools when you get started. Don't even think of buying stuff when it's already here." It was nice of him to offer, and I felt a little better about him.

Mr. Wilson stood on the dock waving as we pulled away. As soon as we were away from the island I looked at Joe and said, "It was depressing enough not to reach our island without hearing all the negative comments back there."

Joe looked at me, and we remembered the sounds we'd heard through the whole conversation. We began to laugh and could hardly stop. "Promise me we'll never get that uninhibited," I pleaded.

We headed straight to a large island in the channel. Joe pointed up the rocky slope. "Mercedes and his family live up there."

I could see three children waving as they scampered up the porous rocks. Another child was carrying a huge silver-colored container on her head. A young man and woman were fishing from a dugout and waved to us as we pulled up alongside a larger one. I could smell a fire and something cooking.

"*Hola!*" Joe called out as he stopped the engine. "*Está Mercedes aquí?*" he asked one of the children. They had all stopped in their tracks and were staring at the two of us.

"*Su papa?*" Joe asked again. The children giggled shyly. About fifteen feet above us a voice called down, "*Señor José?*"

I looked up and saw a man combing his slick black hair into place. His piercing black eyes were aglow with recognition. *So this is Mercedes*, I thought, looking at the islander who would help us build our home. He scampered down the rocks with the agility of a mountain goat.

Around the multicolored patches, his pants were blue polyester, and his shirt was a paisley print buttoned only at the waist. He wore no shoes, and his feet were scarred and rough. The bottoms looked thicker than my Keds.

But his face was friendly and warm. He stuck out his calloused, worn hands toward Joe, and they laughed and exchanged greetings.

Joe took my arm and introduced me. Mercedes summoned his children and wife to his side as an army general would call his troops for inspection. They began to gather around, smoothing their hair and standing at attention. The group grew larger until finally there were seven children standing on the rocks. Then Mercedes' wife appeared in a clean white apron. She smiled a toothless grin and laughed jovially, her round tummy shaking. She, too, was barefoot.

Mercedes introduced them. His oldest son, Enrique, had on the only pair of shoes. Then Marta Eugenia, Teresa, Rosa, Carlita, Maria and Mercedes II. And then the mama, Rosa Elena.

They all giggled when Joe told them my name. "Sandy," they said with a perfect short "a." Joe told me they thought it funny that my name sounded like *sandia* which is the Spanish word for watermelon. When I tried to say all their names, there were more giggles, including my own.

We climbed the steep cliff to the upper part of their island. "Mercedes and his family are just squatters on this property," Joe explained. "It's actually owned by the same family that owns our island. Mercedes takes care of it and keeps the coconuts harvested for the owners."

At the top of the cliff, the hard-packed earth had been swept smooth and sprinkled with water. A thatched-roof shack perched amidst the huge rocks. Another bamboo-framed shelter covered the cooking area. Among fish fins and tails scattered on the rocks to dry in the sun, Mercedes pulled up a small footstool, apparently the only seat, and motioned for me to sit down. The children stared at me and giggled shyly.

Joe explained our problem to Mercedes. They were both gesturing as much as talking. Joe interpreted what I couldn't understand. "He thinks we should try to find another island."

"Oh, no," I said trying not to sound too upset in front of all these people. "What about the house—you've designed it for that island! What about the deposit we sent the owner over a year ago? What will we do?"

The children giggled again. Apparently, my Tennessee accent must have made my English even more fascinating for them. Mercedes' black eyes flashed as he rattled off some Spanish even Joe couldn't understand. The children snapped to attention.

I smiled, hoping they realized I understood. I was still trying to absorb the reality of this family. Proud, dignified, and curious, they had already won my heart. We had just left two Americans who had everything and yet were so unhappy, and here was this island family with practically nothing and yet so content!

Joe finally filled me in on the rest of their discussion. "Tomorrow we'll have to go to town and see Señora Marin about the island. Mercedes will show us where she lives."

"You never mentioned Señora Marin," I said.

"I never met her," Joe replied. "I dealt with her son. Mercedes is going to take us to another island near here so we can set up camp until we work something out."

"Great! At least, we'll be out of the camper and can use our new tent!"

We stood up to leave. "*Adios*," chorused the children as they stood on the rocks waving.

Mercedes rode with us to a big island about a mile away. Tomme Terra was lush with mango trees. From it we could see our "dream island" shimmering in the water about a mile further out.

Surely it will be ours after all, I thought wistfully as we docked the boat at a clearing and followed a path through the underbrush to a large clearing in the center of the island. Mercedes was saying something about the mangoes.

"The clearing was made in the mango harvesting last month," Joe explained.

"No doubt about it—this island is beautiful," I exclaimed. "It will be fine until we find out about ours."

"Let's go get the equipment!"

We dropped off Mercedes at his island, then headed the three miles to Puerto Asese. It took over an hour to unload the camping supplies and decide what we would need for a temporary campsite.

Our necessities made quite a load. Of course, we needed the tent and bed out of the truck. After the dock manager helped move our plywood kitchen aboard, the boat was full.

I was getting concerned about the time. Mercedes and Mr. Wilson had warned us about the afternoon wind that turned the gentle waves of the lake into high seas.

"Let's go, Joe."

"Okay, check one more time. If we forget something, we have to do without it."

We were finally on our way, moving as fast as possible without splashing all our belongings. I hoped Joe remembered the route. I wasn't sure I'd even recognize which island was Tomme Terre.

It seemed to me that the waves were getting choppier with each passing moment.

We'd been away from the dock for about an hour when Joe finally admitted he wasn't sure where we were.

I stared at him. "You're kidding, aren't you?"

"No, I've somehow missed a turn."

I stared at Mombachu towering behind him. "Hey, aren't we too close to the mountain? Shouldn't we be farther east?"

Joe squinted up at the mountain behind us. "I think you're right. It's worth a try, anyway."

We plowed through the now-seething water. It sprayed on either side of us as we bounced across wave after wave.

"Isn't that the Wilsons'?" I asked pointing to the right.

Joe sat up on the edge of his seat in a spray of water. "Oh, good, now I know how to get there."

Mercedes' island came into view a few minutes later, and from there we easily found Tomme Terre.

"Good thing you noticed the distance from the mountain," Joe said as we unloaded our wet supplies.

I beamed with pride.

Three hours later we had a real campsite. Our regal yellow and blue tent stood beneath the elegant palms. The plywood kitchen was set up near a spot cleared for the fire. A fallen coconut tree would be our dining room bench. Joe gathered dry branches for the fire while I swept the dirt outside the tent with a palm frond and sprinkled it with water to keep down the dust.

It was getting dark when we stopped to admire our labor. "How about this, woman?" Joe said. "Ain't this paradise?!"

I walked to him and put my arms around him. Just then we heard someone call out, *"Señor José, Señor Jose."*

We looked toward the path. It was Mercedes coming to check on us and bringing two tin plates, one on top of the other. He handed them to me and explained, "Rosa Elena, she thought you need."

I know my face showed my surprise as I thanked him, *"Gracias, gracias!"*

He was obviously very curious about our camp, so Joe showed him around. He walked over to our tent and the plywood kitchen and gently touched everything, admiring things he had never seen.

After a little while he said, *"Buenas noches,"* and started down the path to his tiny five-foot dugout. As he rowed away, he called out, *"Hasta mañana."*

I ran back to the two plates he'd brought. As I turned over the top plate my mouth began to water. Joe walked up, flashed his light on the contents, and said, "Yech—look at that shiny eye looking at me!"

"You mean you don't like fish?" I exclaimed.

"Not when it's staring at me," he shrugged.

"Well, it looks delicious to me," I said, reaching for a fork. The rice beneath the fish was delicately seasoned, and the tomatoes and onions on top of the black fish were delicious.

Joe just sat staring at his plate. "You want me to cut the head off for you?" I asked.

"Oh, that's okay," he answered weakly. "I'll try it."

I was licking the bones as Joe picked at his. "Want me to heat up some soup for you?" I offered, hoping he'd say no since I'd have to get out the stove, prime it, mess up a pan, and end up washing a lot more dishes.

"Do you mind?" he asked. How could I have resisted those pleading eyes? Besides, what else did I have to do anyway?

He got the kerosene lantern going in just a few minutes and a little while later enjoyed his soup and sandwich while I finished his fish. I stacked all the dirty plates and pan and put them beside the kitchen. "Joe, I'd rather wait til morning to wash these. Do you think they'll be all right?"

"Sure, it's almost eight o'clock, anyway. Time for bed if we're going with Mercedes in the morning."

Joe reached for the lantern and went to check the boat one more time. We wanted to be sure it wasn't hitting any rocks. Small and alone, I stood in the darkness staring up at the palm branches high above.

"Everything's okay," he said as he stumbled back up the path.

"Look up." I motioned to the sky. Joe turned off the lantern. "Oh, Sandy, look," he exclaimed pointing upward, "A falling star!"

We watched as the streak of light plummeted toward earth. "I've never seen so many stars," I said.

"It's incredible," Joe agreed.

We were both surprised, too, at how noisy it was. Waves were rolling in and crashing on the rocks nearby. It sounded as if all the frogs in the world were singing their nightly song. "And I thought island life would be peaceful and quiet!"

"Come on," Joe said. "Let's go to bed."

The next morning we were up at dawn. Our dishes from the night before were covered with ants. I decided I'd better add bug spray to our shopping list.

I got the Coleman stove going and surprised Joe with blueberry pancakes for breakfast. The milk had stayed cold in the cooler for two days, but we needed another block of ice. We sat on the coconut tree and ate in silence. There was so much to think about for our shopping trip, and we were both apprehensive about meeting Señora Marin.

It was about 8 A.M. when we stopped for Mercedes. He showed us a new, shorter route through the islands to the dock. He cautioned us both to stay exactly on course because of the danger of hitting rocks hidden below the surface. He described each point of reference: a certain tree there, a large boulder here, a four-by-four post jutting up from a submerged rock.

It seemed impossible to remember it all. I almost asked Joe to forget it and take the longer route until I calculated how much gas we were saving.

An hour later the three of us stood before an imposing wooden door waiting for someone to answer our knock. The door opened and a tiny, gray-haired woman eyed us suspiciously. "Señora Marín?" Joe ventured.

She straightened up and lifted her chin slightly. *"Sí."*

Mercedes stood silently with his hat in his hands, his eyes riveted to the sidewalk. The proud man I'd met the day before was reduced to a shy victim of discrimination. He knew a poor island squatter was not welcome in the home of the rich landowner. Speaking to Joe, he went to the truck. Joe grimaced as he walked away. The impact of classism rolled over me in a wave of understanding.

Señora Marín motioned for us to come in and have a seat. I smiled cordially and tried to dispel my nagging fears. She didn't seem very interested as Joe explained our problem. Suddenly her face changed, and she began to shake her head.

"No . . ." I understood that word and dreaded the interpretation of the rest of her statement.

Joe's face turned red as he spoke calmly to me, "She says her son was wrong. She has no island for sale, nor will she sell any."

"But," I stammered, "I though *Dr.* Marín wanted to sell you an island."

"He does, but she's his mother, and she has the final say about family land."

My stomach collapsed and my heart pounded. While I watched help-lessly, Joe used every persuasive talent he had. It was no use. She would not be won over.

My worst fears had now become reality. Joe *had* overlooked a few details. *Now what?*

We slid silently into the truck beside Mercedes. Then Joe said optimistically, "She's not the only person in Nicaragua who owns an island. We'll just camp on Tomme Terre until we find another one."

I couldn't speak. All I could think was, *What am I doing here?*

SEVEN

Shopping for an Island

Ten days later we were still searching, chasing after a lost dream. One island was advertised for ten thousand dollars—too much. Another belonged to the president of the country and wasn't for sale. We kept running into dead ends.

Day by day the rainy season approached. Then, unexpectedly, as usual, Mercedes dropped by with news of an island.

Joe was enthused immediately. I held back my optimism until I heard more. We asked our standard questions: "Where is it?" "Whose is it?" and "What's the price?"

Mercedes shrugged his shoulders. He seemed no more optimistic than I was but he agreed to show us. We followed him down the path to our boat. "Which way?" Joe asked. Mercedes pointed in the direction of the tiny island in the heart of the channel, only about a mile away. We had passed it often in the past twelve days.

"That one?" I exclaimed. "Except for the coconut trees and that huge fig tree over the water, it has to be the ugliest island of all!"

"Let's at least go look at it and talk to the owner," Joe pleaded. I sensed he wasn't that impressed with it either.

Mercedes pointed out a place to tie the boat and we jumped out onto a huge boulder. We climbed the steep bank, grasping at roots for a hand hold. I looked up at the cluster of coconuts above my head. There were dozens of them, golden ripe and ready to be picked.

I felt as if the breath had been knocked out of me for days. How could Joe have made such a careless mistake? Our plans for the house, the money we'd saved, all our dreams had revolved around the island he'd chosen fifteen months earlier.

We walked around huge black rocks and scraggy trees. This island seemed desolate except for the seven palms swaying gently above us.

"Joe, look at it!" I demanded.

He refused to comment. He was studying the three massive boulders that dominated the island. This island would require much more work.

I climbed up on the largest boulder at one end of the island and surveyed the scene below. The dry soil blew in dusty clouds as the wind whistled in my ears. Rock-filled water surrounded us. At our camp on Tomme Terra a half-mile away, our yellow and blue tent stood out among the lush vegetation. In the other direction was our inaccessible dream island. In the water below a small four-foot dugout plowed through the water toward us.

Mercedes climbed down the rocks and welcomed a tiny Nicaraguan. Across the island I saw his toothless grin and waved half-heartedly in greeting. He was the owner Mercedes told us about. I sat down on my rocky perch and stared at the boulder's bumpy surface.

Joe joined me. "I believe it will work," he said surveying the island.

I stared at him piercingly. Before I could speak, he shoved the end of a tape measure into my hand. "Hold this. I'm going to see if the house will fit."

He scrambled over and around the boulders and let out a cheer. "It will work. This is it!"

Mercedes stood with the Nicaraguan who owned the island. They were grinning and nodding their heads.

I jumped down and made my way to them, but I paid little or no attention to Mercedes' introduction. "What about all these dead trees?" I asked.

Their faces had a puzzled expression. I turned to Joe and with exasperation said, "They don't understand my Spanish. Ask them about these ugly trees, will you?"

He pointed at the trees and rattled off some Spanish. Both the men shouted, "*No, señor!* They are not dead. They only sleep until the time is right for fruit."

Joe and I looked at each other in surprise. "Fruit?"

The owner of the island ran to another type of tree. "*Flores—muy bonitas.*"

We couldn't believe it. Flowers, too!

"When?" we both chorused.

"*Abril*," they answered proudly.

My attitude changed. Just three more months and the island would be beautiful! Graceful coconut trees and fruits and flowers would make it beautiful!

"Oh, Joe, I'm sorry I was so negative. Ask him how much he wants for it."

There we stood, two Nicaraguan men and a young gringo and his wife, haggling over the price of an island as if it were a used car. The owner gave a price, and before Joe could say yes or no, he lowered it! The slightest hesitation or questioning look brought the price lower. Finally, the man asked Joe, "How much will you give me?"

My head felt light with elation. Already he wanted two thousand dollars less than we had planned to spend for our first-choice island.

"What do you think we should offer?" Joe consulted with me. I thought for a second and said, "*Catorce mil cordobas*—two thousand dollars."

The man's hand came to his chest as he spoke, "You try to take away an old man's pleasure! *Dieciseis mil cordobas* makes it yours."

Twenty-three hundred dollars! Joe grabbed the man's hand and shook it wildly. "Okay, *es mio!*"

It was done! We were going to buy an island for a price lower than we'd ever dreamed. We tried not to be too excited as we ran from one tree to another asking its identity.

"When can we make it official?" I asked. We wanted to hire a lawyer to draw up the deed and be sure everything was in order.

In his deep monotone, the man answered, "*Mañana.*"

The next day we were happily on our way to the bank to withdraw twenty-three hundred dollars in cash. The multicolored bills of Nicaragua's currency were much more interesting than the green ones in the United States.

In four hours the necessary paper work was complete. Evaristo Joaquin Carillo was now sixteen thousand cordobas richer, and we finally owned an island. As the deed was read to us, we heard the name of our paradise for the first time. *El Corazón*, The Heart!

I had the overwhelming sensation that Joe's mistake had turned into a wonderful blessing. Now, we not only had an island on which to build our dream house but we also had saved twenty-seven hundred dollars! And what better location for two honeymooners than the Heart?

That night at our camp on Tomme Terra we sat on the rocks staring across the water at *El Corazón*. I leaned back in Joe's arms and spoke softly, "She's still ugly, you know."

"Yeah," Joe admitted as he hugged me, "But just give us three weeks, and she'll start shaping up. I can already see the house sitting proudly under those coconut trees. Look at it, Sandy. It's ours—yours and mine."

Suddenly, I spotted something in the rocks. "Did you see something move over there?"

Joe jumped to his feet and craned his neck to see. "I think so," he answered as he ran to get the binoculars.

I kept watching and tried to figure out what the white creature might be.

Joe came back and we focused in on the mysterious visitor. "It's a little white cat," he said as he handed me the binoculars.

"Oh, isn't she skinny?" I crooned. "Wonder what she eats? How did she get there? Oh, I can't wait til tomorrow!"

The cat scampered down the rocks and into the darkness of a small cave. At dark we finally stopped waiting for her to reappear and strolled back up the path to the tent. "Tomorrow I'll clear a space for the tent and make a shelter for cooking," Joe said as we got ready for bed.

"I can't wait to see that cat again," I said eagerly. "I wonder if she'll come to us."

We snuggled under the sheet and looked up through the screened window at the stars.

"Oh, Joe," I whispered, "sometimes I feel so small, so insignificant, in this huge universe. I really can't believe I'm here in your arms on an island so far from home."

I could feel Joe's heart beating against my back. "Do you know what I mean?"

"I love you," he whispered, kissing the back of my neck. "Sandy, I couldn't do this without you."

The next morning we were up with the sun. I cooked breakfast while Joe made a list of tools we needed to borrow from Mr. Wilson. He had said we could use his house jacks if we needed them, and we definitely would.

"Do you want to go over to *Corazón* with me?" Joe asked.

"I'd like to, but I'd better get the clothes and sheets washed and everything organized for the move."

"It will be our first day apart since we've been married," Joe laughed. "Can you believe it?"

It was the truth! For five weeks we had never been separated longer than thirty minutes. "Of course, I can still see you all day. All I have to do is get the binoculars!"

After breakfast, Joe loaded the shovel, the rake, and a machete into the boat. When he was ready to leave, I walked him out to the rocks where the boat was docked. "Do you have your briefcase, dear?" I asked jokingly. "And don't forget to call around lunch and let me know what time you'll be home for supper."

He grinned and pulled me close. "You just watch out for the wild natives all day—you never know what we might do!"

I watched him drive the boat over to our island, and then turned to my housekeeping chores.

I'd seen the women on other islands washing their clothes on rocks. Surely, if they could do it, I could learn how.

I unzipped the tent and gathered our bundle of dirty clothes and the sheets. As I picked up the foam rubber mattress we'd been sleeping on, a four-inch scorpion arched its tail at me. I shrieked, quickly stomped it, picked it up with a stick, and threw it into the hot coals of our breakfast fire.

When I returned to the tent, I shook each piece of clothing violently, just in case. Cautiously, I searched all around our bed, inside the potty, and in every fold of the tent floor until I was satisfied no other creatures had invaded our domain.

This was my first experience with a live scorpion, and I kept conjuring up visions of old late-night horror movies. "Thank God I had my shoes on," I said to myself. From now on I'd be shaking them, too, each time I started to put them on.

I dropped the clothes onto the rocks and ran back to get the detergent. The water felt great as I stepped into the lake. It was only about 8 A.M. but already the temperature must have been in the lower nineties. I picked up a pair of Joe's undershorts, sprinkled some detergent on them, and began to scrub. "Now this is love," I sang, making up a little song.

Someone giggled. I started and looked around. Two little girls stared at me from a dugout a few yards away. They were busy fishing. Their dark black eyes shone when I said, *"Hola."* They giggled and returned my greeting.

The bigger of the two must have been about seven years old. She began to paddle, and they waved good-by as they disappeared behind another island.

These children were out on the lake alone without life jackets. That would never happen in Tennessee! *How different life is for kids here,* I thought.

The water was cloudy with detergent, and my skin was coated with the soapy film. In a few minutes the waves had replenished my fresh water supply for rinsing our clothes. I had put off the sheets until last because they would be so heavy.

My arms were exhausted as I laid everything on the underbrush to dry. It had taken over an hour just to wash and rinse our clothes. I thought wistfully of the automation I'd taken for granted at home.

I reached for the binoculars and focused on *El Corazón.* Joe was hammering and chopping something. I felt lonely without his company, yet satisfied that I'd managed to do the dreaded laundry.

Loud screeches interrupted my thoughts. A flock of parrots had landed in the coconut trees above my head. Their nervous chattering was deafening. I stood motionless staring at their brilliant colors. After a few moments they hurried on to another island.

I glanced around the camp site and realized I had too much to do to stand around all day. Cleaning the tent was next.

First, the potty had to be emptied and cleaned. I carried it to the far side of the island and flung the contents into the lake. Hundreds of fish covered the surface of the water. It was like watching piranha devouring their prey. The fishermen with their fancy boats on the TVA lakes at home would never believe the bounty of this lake.

After disinfecting the potty and tent floor, I had to start on our big meal of the day. Each meal required gathering firewood and carrying and boiling water before I could even start to cook. Every meal was a challenge. *But,* I thought, *tomorrow is moving day!*

I had potatoes, carrots, and onions boiling with some beef the Wilsons had sent over when I heard Joe's whistle and the boat motor. I responded with a loud "Ouuu-whoop!"

Exhilarated, he jumped from the boat.

"Did you see that cat?" I asked.

"No." He buried his face in my hair as he pulled me into his arms. "Oh, Sandy, it's happening now. It really is our dream island, after all."

Suddenly, he snatched me up in his arms, carried me to the water's edge, and jumped in. After a swim we climbed up on the rocks and walked back up the path.

The cooking fire was just about out, and only a little bit of water remained around the vegetables and meat. "You're lucky this time," I laughed. "You almost lost your dinner."

Joe talked through the meal and long after we were in bed. The last thing I remember before I dropped off to sleep was hearing him say, "Tomorrow we'll move *home* to our very own island!"

EIGHT

Our Mysterious Creature

"Señor José, Señor José!" Mercedes' voice called through the early morning darkness.

"What time is it?" I asked sleepily while Joe fumbled for his watch.

"Five-thirty! Let's get moving. I told Mercedes to bring his big dugout to help. Let's pack up and go."

I was pulling on my cut-offs and a top as fast as I could. Joe scrambled into his swim trunks and met Mercedes at the path. *It's going to take some time to get used to unexpected visitors,* I thought. Of course, how could people possibly let us know they were coming? I laughed as I imagined working out some jungle drum signal. The tour boat owners would probably like the idea.

"Sandy, hurry up," Joe called. "Let's eat something quick and get going. We've got to carry several loads from the truck to the island."

I stepped outside the tent and zipped it behind me. Mercedes was sitting on our dining room coconut tree sporting his mischievous grin.

He stood up and greeted me. *"Buenos días."*

I answered, *"Hola,"* as I pulled my hair back into a pony tail.

Quickly, we smeared butter on four slices of bread, peeled some bananas and oranges, poured some milk, and sat down to eat.

Joe looked upward and asked God to bless the food as he had done countless times in the past. Then he leaned over for a quick kiss.

We had promised each other that we'd begin every meal together in this way—a prayer to thank God for the food we shared and the kiss to ensure we'd have to work out any problems between us before we could eat. Our promise had already been challenged several times, but so far, we both had been too hungry to insist on our own stubborn way and had apologized and made up before we ate together.

Joe offered Mercedes some bread and fruit. He gladly accepted, and we ate quickly.

The palm trees began to sway as a gentle breeze joined the first rays of the sun filtering through the trees.

Joe stood up and stretched. "You ready?" he asked as he went to the tent for his toothbrush.

I looked around our campsite one last time. "Yep!" I answered and followed.

Mercedes, who used a twig to pick at his teeth, laughed at the sight of our frothing mouths.

Soon we were busy carrying everything to the boat.

By the time we had everything loaded, there was no room in our boat for me. I climbed in the dugout with Mercedes and sat on top of our foam rubber mattress to keep it from blowing away.

We headed toward *El Corazón* without so much as a glance back at the beautiful island we had called home for the past two weeks.

We pulled alongside a huge, smooth-faced boulder and began to unload. "We'll build some steps beside this coconut tree," Joe said as we struggled up the root-filled bank.

On the top level of the island, I stared in surprise at a bamboo-framed shelter under the spreading branches of what we'd been told was a fruit tree.

Joe set down his armload of equipment and ran over to the roofless frame. "Here's your kitchen and dining room until the house is finished!" he said proudly. "The tarp we bought at the garage-sale last summer will make a good roof." He looked at me expectantly. "Well, what do you think?"

I walked toward him. "You forgot one thing," I teased. "If you can decide where the threshold is around here . . ."

His eyes twinkled as he swept me up in his arms and carried me between two supporting posts. We looked up at the sky and laughed. Mercedes stood beneath a coconut tree with his arms full—staring at us with a puzzled expression.

"He'll never figure us out," Joe said as he set me down.

The rest of the morning I cleared a place for the tent. Mercedes gathered fallen palm branches and showed me how to make a fine broom. Then I tried to sweep all the tiny gravel from the spot we had chosen beside the bamboo frame.

By noon, we had the tent set up, a clothesline stretched around three coconut trees on the south end of the island, and an area designated for trash burning.

I opened a can of soup for lunch while Joe gathered some kindling. One of Mercedes' daughters, Carlita, rowed up with his lunch. She handed him three tins stacked one upon another. He had beans, rice, plantano, and a jar of coffee to wash the food down. My mouth watered as I got the fire going to heat our soup.

"I sure am thirsty," Joe said as we tried not to watch Mercedes eat.

I glanced at the luscious coconuts above us. "I wonder if those are any good."

Joe walked to the bottom of a tree. "Let's just find out," he said as he hugged the tree and started climbing. Mercedes stopped eating and watched closely. When Joe was about twelve feet up the tree, his shoe slipped and he scraped his belly on the way back down. He was panting from the exertion.

Mercedes was trying his best not to laugh, and so was I.

"Well, I'd have made it except for my shoe!" Joe insisted.

"*Amigo*," Mercedes scolded, "if you want a coconut, I'll be glad to get it for you."

I didn't want Joe to get hurt any worse, so I quickly insisted, "*Sí, por favor.*"

Mercedes grabbed the tree and scampered up the trunk—barefooted, of course, since he had no shoes. He got to the top of the thirty-foot tree in seconds and perched on a swaying branch. He had a short machete and chopped off four golden beauties.

Before we could ask him how we would catch the huge things, he had tossed them out into the lake. They bobbed to the surface, and Joe scrambled down the rocks to retrieve them.

Mercedes descended as quickly as he had gone up, dusted his hands, and sat back down to eat. His breathing hadn't changed.

"You've got to teach me how," Joe pleaded with him. I, too, wanted to learn though I could imagine going up much more readily than coming back down.

Our soup was ready. Mercedes chopped off the tops of two coconuts, and we had our first taste of coco water.

"I can't believe how these fibers keep the inside so cool," Joe said as the clear liquid dripped from his chin.

"Me either," I answered. "I thought it would be like milk, but it's more like sweet water."

Mercedes cut a piece of the white meat from the inside of the nut. He handed the soft, wet pulp to me. It didn't taste like coconut. It was too watery.

"Where does real coconut come from?" I asked.

He laughed and pointed to a dark brown, speckled nut lying on the ground. When I looked at him questioningly, he hopped up and began chopping it with his machete. The tough fibers clung to the dark brown shell inside. He finally got to the nut and whacked it with his machete, splitting it open. Inside was the hard, white meat I was accustomed to. He carved out a hunk for me.

"Delicious!" I exclaimed. Joe, too, was reaching for some.

As we finished eating, we realized we had better get a move on or we weren't going to be able to run all our errands in town before dark. We still had to go by the Wilsons' for some tools he was going to loan us, get a few groceries, buy gas for the boat, and finish setting up our camp.

Joe called for Mercedes and asked him to begin stacking rock for a dock while we were gone. That was a necessity before we could haul all the building supplies. After giving him instructions, we grabbed the cooler and our supply list and were ready to go when I remembered I'd better put on a skirt. I had learned that although the weather felt like a Tennessee summer, a woman in Central America dresses conservatively if she doesn't want to be harassed in public.

We waved good-by to Mercedes and headed for the Wilsons' to give them our latest news.

As we pulled up to their dock, we heard the now familiar cry of Bea's raspy voice, "You kids want some Kool-Aid?"

Len was down at their chicken house stomping around in the high-topped rubber boots he always wore outside the house. "Be up in a minute," he called.

We went into the house and sat at their picnic table. Bea handed us two glasses of the Clorox-smelling liquid. She had told me she always added a small amount of Clorox to their water to help kill the germs when she boiled it.

"Well," she struggled to get her breath, "how is island hunting coming along?"

"We moved this morning," I answered enthusiastically. "You must come see it. It's beautiful."

Len was on the porch, taking off his boots and putting on his flip-flops. "Don't say any more until I can hear it," he called. He came on into the house. "Dern boa ate one of my chicks," he muttered angrily. "How are you two getting along? We were getting worried about you. Haven't heard from you in a few days."

"We moved to our island this morning, and we love it," Joe answered.

"Where is it? Sure hope it's not too far out, or the launch owners will charge you double for hauling supplies and visitors to your place."

"Really?" I asked. I had discovered he could really exaggerate about things he wasn't sure of. But this was good news if he was right.

"*El Corazón* is in the heart of the channel just past Mercedes' island," Joe answered, "just about two or three miles from here."

"I'll get Leonso to bring me over soon," Len said referring to the islander who lived next to the Wilsons. Leonso had helped Len and Bea since their arrival, and one of his thirteen children, Mario, was practically Mr. Wilson's shadow. In exchange for meals, he helped clean the house, garden, feed the animals, and wash clothes. As we talked, the young boy came to the door and waited.

Bea shouted, "Okay, Mario." He came in and proudly spoke to Joe and me.

"Hello, my name Mario. Like here?"

I looked at his close-cropped black hair. He was grinning from ear to ear. All he had on was an old pair of lavender cut-off polyester slacks with an elasticized waistband. Evidently, they had been Bea's.

Joe answered his question in Spanish. "Yes, we love Nicaragua. I'm Joe and this is my wife, Sandy."

"*Mucho gusto*," I replied as I had learned in the past few weeks.

He was very surprised that we spoke any Spanish. Evidently the Wilsons had not learned much of the language since they were only in town two mornings a week and Mario always accompanied them on their shopping trips. They really had little reason to learn the language, but I was still shocked that they could make a new country their home and not want to communicate with the people.

Len and Bea encouraged us to hire Mario's father to help with the rock moving. "He's moved a lot for me around here," Len said. "He's a hard worker. I'll loan you my steel bar to help bust up smaller ones and use as a lever. And you'll need my house jacks—I've got two, a fifteen-tonner and a twenty-tonner. How much are you planning to pay these two men, anyway?"

"I told Mercedes that I would pay him fifteen cordobas a day and he'd have to bring his lunch," Joe answered.

"Fifteen cordobas is way too much!" Len said angrily. "You'll ruin these men. They're not used to making that kind of money. Next thing, they'll start insisting that the rest of us pay them that much! Ten cordobas with their noon meal provided is the usual amount, twelve if they furnish their own food."

Joe and I had already discussed all this and dreaded having to justify our decision to someone else. Fifteen cordobas was only $2.14 a day! These men were going to be doing back-breaking labor beginning at 6:30 A.M. and ending at 2:30 P.M. each day with some overtime until the boulders were removed. I felt bad enough about paying such wages but knew we were being more than generous by the local standards.

Joe tried to explain our position to the Wilsons, but they wouldn't listen. They just kept arguing that we were going to ruin the local economy.

Finally, Joe stood up. "This isn't getting us anywhere. We've got a lot to do today and we're not going to change our minds about this. Thanks so much for the Kool-Aid, Bea. We better be going."

Len stood up and said, "Come on, I'll loan you those tools, anyway, but I'm telling you these people will take advantage of you if you pay them too much."

Joe followed him down to their tool shed. I was so glad Joe hadn't lost his temper. He seemed to be able to stay calm through anything.

Bea struggled for breath. "You two kids listen to the radio?" she asked.

"We really haven't taken the time," I answered.

"Well, you've just got to tune in the Voice of America each evening. Otherwise, you won't know what's going on in the world. Come here."

I followed her to her bedside. They had a battery-powered radio. She

showed me where to tune in for the broadcast at six o'clock each evening.

"You listen in and you'll see just how happy you are to be away from
that godforsaken country of ours."

I heard Joe yelling my name. Relieved, I said good-by, but before I
could go she said, "You two stop back by and I'll have your supper for
you."

I hesitated a moment, but she insisted they would love for us to come
by. "You're going to be worn out after an afternoon in Granada, anyway."

She was right, and I did so want a night off from cooking. I opened the
screen and called to Joe, "Bea insists we come back for supper. Is it
okay?"

He glared at me with one of his looks and nodded.

I turned and said, "Okay, see you later."

We sped across the water toward the dock. "Don't do that to me
again," Joe said.

"But, Joe," I insisted, "I'm so tired of cooking and trying to think of
something to fix all the time. Please understand. I look forward to eating
someone else's cooking and having the night off."

Every time we left the Wilsons we felt depressed. It angered me to
realize how manipulative they could be. Thinking of Mario made me
even madder. He had been with them every day for four years and still
couldn't write his own name.

"I'd give anything to know fluent Spanish now," I moaned, hitting the
seat with my fist. "These island children deserve better than this."

"Calm down," Joe replied. "You can't change things overnight. Let's
get the house finished, and by then, you'll know more about these people and what you can do to help them."

He was right, of course.

"For now," he continued, "just hope we've listed everything we need
and that we can get back to our island before dark."

We arrived at Puerto Asese and parked our boat between two tourist
launches. Joe unhooked the gas tank so we could fill it in town. Then he
got the cooler and put it in the back of our truck.

"All this loading and unloading kind of gets to me sometimes," I com-
plained.

Joe's head jerked, and he glared at me. "You may as well get used to it 'cause that's the way it is!"

We were silent as we drove the three miles into Granada. The streets were filled with children on their way home from school. We bumped along the unpaved road until we got to paved streets in the center of town. There was garbage in the gutters on either side of us, and as we passed the slaughterhouse, I almost gagged from the smell.

"Will I ever get used to this?" I said under my breath.

I only hoped we had some mail waiting at the Post Office. We pulled up in front of the gleaming white-columned building and I rushed in. The women at the windows inside greeted me and closed for lunch. It was one o'clock. I rushed to our box and peeked in. Nothing. *Nothing!* I felt crushed. We hadn't had mail all week. I walked slowly back to the truck where Joe was asking someone directions.

He turned to me and glanced at my face. "No mail, huh?" he asked sympathetically. "Don't worry about it. We'll probably have to come in tomorrow and we'll check then."

We drove down some back streets until we came to a little concrete house where the blacksmith lived. We needed to have a steel bar sharpened and we took it inside where the family was eating lunch. Joe said we could come back later, but the man insisted he would be glad to help him. After examining the steel bar, the man nodded, "*Sí*, I can fix it. Come back at 3:30."

Next we went on to the market. It was a mess. Not many vendors were left, and the fruits and vegetables were wilted and bruised. I returned to the truck with only a couple dozen limes.

"What are you doing?" Joe asked when he saw my purchase. "We've got to have food for tomorrow morning."

"I'll just have to buy what we need at the little grocery store near the park." I wouldn't look at Joe as I spoke. I just couldn't make myself walk through the slimy garbage in the market again.

We went around the block and stopped at the store. The owner was happy to see me, and she helped me find the things I needed.

Then we went on to the ice house and purchased a huge block of ice to keep our milk cold. Joe hardly spoke. I knew he was disappointed in me, but I refused to go in the market again.

Finally, we picked up the now-sharpened steel bar, bought gasoline, and headed back to Puerto Asese. I would be relieved to get back to the island. It was so hot my skin was damp with perspiration.

We bumped along the road and arrived at the dock by four o'clock. Chico, the boy who worked at the refreshment stand, called to us.

I hopped down into the boat with my little bag of groceries and saw Joe hand Chico some money.

"What was that for?" I asked.

"We have to pay the dock fee at the first of each month," Joe answered as he loaded the cooler, a few tools from a hardware store, and the gas tank.

We waved good-by to Chico and headed for the Wilsons' island. The lake was filled with choppy waves in the afternoon wind. I could feel tension draining away from me.

"Joe," I said cautiously, "please don't be mad at me. I'm sorry I couldn't shop in the market. I just can't stand the filth. Please understand."

"Let's not talk about it right now," he said calmly. "We're tired and hungry. I'm sure we'll feel better when we get back to our island."

We arrived at the Wilsons', and she shouted for us to hurry. "Supper's ready!"

We hurried up the steps and went in. She had prepared a wonderful supper of salad and spaghetti. "This is delicious," I complimented.

"You like venison?" she said as she struggled for a breath.

"Is this venison?" I asked. "It tastes great."

"It's lots better than the venison I grew up on," Joe said.

"Where did you find all these beautiful vegetables?" I asked.

"In the market."

"You mean you buy all your food in the native market in Granada?" I asked unbelievingly.

Len explained proudly. "It's important to do your shopping early in the morning, before eight in the morning. That's the only way to get things fresh. You two must get used to Central American ways."

Joe glanced at me and smiled. "You mean the market is clean in the morning?"

"Oh, yes," Len replied. "I couldn't stomach the mess in the afternoon. And you must find the vendors who will treat you fairly. Once they see you're not a tourist, you'll get prices that you won't believe!" Joe squeezed my hand.

I was so relieved. I was anxious for tomorrow morning just to discover the "real" market of Granada. We had so much to learn.

Mario cleared the table for us, and we all sat down to listen to the Voice of America. It was wonderful to hear English and know we could tune in at least once a day to a program we could understand.

After the broadcast, Joe stood up. "Well, I hate to eat and run, but we'd better go before it gets any darker."

We thanked Bea for the scrumptious meal and hurried to the boat. It was the first time we had visited with them and left in good spirits.

As we skimmed along the water toward our island, the sun was slowly disappearing behind us. *El Corazón* shone like an emerald in the channel before us, her palm trees a brilliant green in the last rays of the sun. Then we saw that flash of white fur again. In the hustle and bustle I'd forgotten about our mysterious creature.

By lantern light we unloaded everything quickly and fastened the tarp on our makeshift kitchen.

About 7:30 Joe got hungry for a snack and got out some crackers with peanut butter. As he sat on the rocks eating, our little visitor crept up from below. We sat very quietly, waiting to see if the little cat would come any closer. Joe dropped a piece of cracker, and she jumped. We froze.

She looked at us and took one cautious step in our direction. As we waited, she came closer and closer.

Finally, she grabbed the piece of cracker and scampered away to a safer distance. Joe dropped another piece, and she stared at it intently.

"I wonder what she's been eating," I said quietly.

The cat cocked her head to one side and looked at me.

"Look at her eyes!" Joe whispered. "They're two different colors!"

Even in the lantern light we could see the cat had one green eye and one blue eye. I was already thinking of a name for her.

"What do you want to call her?" Joe asked.

I thought of the Spanish word for cat, *Gato. No,* I thought, *I want it to end in an "e" sound.* It would be easier to call for her. Suddenly, the name of our island came to mind, *Corazón.*

"What about Cory?" I said it aloud for the first time. I could see the little cat's whiskers twitching as she watched us, keeping an eye on the piece of cracker.

"I'll get some bread and milk," Joe said as he slowly stood up. "Cory" scampered back down in her rock hideaway.

"Oh, you scared her," I cried.

"When she tastes what I'm fixing her," Joe assured me, "she'll be our pet for sure."

He found a can of tuna in the kitchen and dumped the whole thing on a plate. Beside that he poured milk into a bowl. I didn't even fuss about the tuna. I so wanted the little animal to be a pet. I'd always loved cats, and this one was so skinny—it needed our love and attention.

Joe set the two bowls in the dirt beside us. We sat back down to wait.

I couldn't resist giving her name a try so I called, "Cory, come on. Here, Cory."

In a few minutes the little cat reappeared on the rocks a few feet from us. Her nose twitched as she caught the aroma from the tuna. She cautiously moved toward us until she was at the bowls. Quickly snatching a piece of tuna, she moved back a few feet to eat it. She looked at us one more time and went back to the bowls. This time she didn't move as she ate every morsel and lapped up the milk.

I could feel my heart beating with excitement as she looked up at us and licked her face. Then she sauntered over and arched her back as she rubbed Joe's leg. I reached to pet her and she meowed. Cory had become a part of our little family.

I felt contented as we crawled into bed that night. Joe zipped the tent closed. The waves were crashing on the rocks on the far end of the island and the palm branches above us were whispering with the wind.

"Sandy," Joe said as he took me in his arms, "this is paradise." And so it seemed.

NINE

El Corazón

The next morning we heard Mercedes' voice at 6:15. Another full day lay ahead. I wanted to get to the market before eight o'clock as Len had suggested.

Joe went down to the lake and jumped in for a quick bath. I thought how easy life would be if I were a man and didn't have to worry about my hair, my makeup, or who might be watching me bathe.

I hurriedly put on a little mascara and tried to fix my hair with a ribbon. It was no use. It was already so hot, I couldn't stand it on my back so up it went into a scarf. I had only a five- by seven-inch mirror and dreaded to think what I must look like. *Well*, I fussed at myself, *I might as well get used to it*. I thought wistfully of my dressing room at home—of hot, running water, of a big, bubble bath. . . .

"Sandy," I heard Joe calling, "are you about ready?"

I stepped out of the tent and went to our plywood-box kitchen. I couldn't think of anything I could fix quickly. "Joe," I called into the tent where he was dressing, "do you think we can grab something to eat in town?"

"Isn't there something you can fix?" he answered. "I don't want us to start eating out all the time. How about some fruit or something?"

I glanced at the bananas. I felt tired already as I sliced them up and poured milk over them. I didn't even feel hungry this early in the morning.

Joe wolfed down the bananas and milk and ate a slice of bread. "Just leave the bowls until we get back from town."

Gliding toward our island in a small dugout was Leonso, coming to work. He and Mercedes would begin moving the first boulder while we were in town. I couldn't imagine their accomplishing much, but Len had assured us his house jacks would do the trick.

Joe gave the men instructions and we were off. It seemed to me he had been in rapid motion ever since we had purchased *El Corazón*. From dawn to dusk, he was running crazy measuring, marking, checking the plans, and making lists. I was beginning to feel left out.

In town, Joe let me out so he could go buy gloves, cement, and other supplies. The market was wall-to-wall food and people. I pushed through the crowds and was amazed at the variety of fruits and vegetables.

In one section of the market freshly slaughtered meat hung from hooks. The Wilsons had told me the names of the different cuts, but the pieces of meat weren't exactly "cuts." They looked as if they had been torn from the beef and resembled no meat I'd seen in the U.S. I studied and studied the long red strips, but finally turned away and went on to the vegetable vendors.

"Cuánto cuesta?" I asked of the woman in the first stall where I stopped. She was very friendly, but her price was way too much. Bea had instructed me to walk away saying, *"Demasiado."* Sure enough, as I turned, the woman grabbed my arm and lowered her price. It was still higher than the Wilsons had said I should pay. Len had been kind enough to write down reasonable prices on the items I needed, so I knew what the price should be. The woman threw up her hands and didn't want to fool with me any longer.

I hoped that in the future she would see I wasn't a tourist and treat me more fairly. I walked on to another woman up the crowded aisle. She tried the same thing, but I said, *"No soy una tourista—Yo vivo aqui ahora."* Having told her I was no tourist, she understood that I would be a regular customer and treated me fairly. As I picked out my fruit, I noticed there were no bags. I looked at her questioningly. She realized I didn't understand. She pulled some used plastic bags from beneath her stand and indicated that I would need to pay her for them and use them over and over again. I was amazed. I stood and watched other people and noticed for the first time that other shoppers carried their own bags and usually huge, deep baskets as well.

I had also noticed that in the crowded aisles of the market, about the only way to carry anything was on my head. I told the woman to wait a few minutes with my choices of fruits and vegetables and headed for a basket vendor. I felt so proud as I hoisted my brand new basket atop my head and headed back for my purchases.

I asked my newfound merchant-friend her name. "Maria Cecilia," she answered proudly and asked mine.

"Sandy," I answered, and she giggled.

Then, she showed me how to load the basket for easier balancing. As she helped me lift it to my head, she stopped and shook her head. "No, no," she said and asked me something I couldn't understand.

She pulled a round, flattened pile of cloth from beneath her stand and explained that I would need one to pad my head against the basket's weight. I removed my scarf and she stared at my blond hair and touched it. *"Bonito,"* she cried. I thanked her and lifted the basket to my head on top of my scarf pad. I felt like a queen as I made my way back out of the market.

Joe was waiting in the truck. He looked up and smiled. "Well, well," he teased, "I've got a real native wife, now, don't I?"

"When in Rome, do as the Romans do," I laughed back.

"Now let's see just how much you spent."

I began to count the brightly colored cordobas. "This can't be right!" I said, counting them again. "That whole basket of stuff only cost seventeen cordobas and a few centavos. That's only $2.50!"

"I told you we would save lots of money by buying in the market."

"Of course," I admitted, "I didn't buy meat."

Joe looked up and across the street. "Look, there's Mr. Wilson and Mario."

"Oh, great. They can help me buy the rest. I needed help picking out the right parts."

I caught up with them, and Len was more than happy to show me around the meat section of the market. He even introduced me to a man who sold specialty items like apples from Guatemala and even strawberries in season. I was glad to know I could get some familiar foods along with all the new ones.

They walked me back to the truck and I showed Joe my purchases. "I'm proud of you," he said.

"Len says we should buy a meat grinder so we can have ground beef," I said, hoping Joe would agree to the purchase.

"I guess if I want a good hamburger we'd better get one," he admitted as we drove toward the hardware store.

While he was inside, I looked down my list one last time to be sure I had everything. I couldn't believe what I had bought for so little money—a dozen each of oranges, tangerines, bananas, lemons, four peppers, four pounds of potatoes, two pounds of onions, one pound of yard-long green beans, one pineapple, one cantaloupe, ten tomatoes, eight eggs (also in a plastic bag), two pounds of carrots, and fresh rolls! All for $2.50. The meat only cost an additional fifteen cordobas.

We drove back to Puerto Asese and unloaded the truck. Then, we loaded the boat and headed back to the island. It was only nine o'clock in the morning.

Over the roar of the boat motor, I shouted to Joe, "We've done a lot already."

Joe nodded and stood up and danced a little jig on the boat seat. Just at that moment we were passing an island on our route home, and somebody whistled. I glanced around as we sped past and saw a young boy mimic Joe. He wiggled his legs and made a swimming motion with his arms and waved.

I burst out laughing as Joe gave a Tarzan yell. As we watched the island, a dozen children scampered up on the rocks and waved to us till we were out of sight.

"You're crazy," I said laughing till my sides hurt. Joe's face was red as a beet. "You like to show off until somebody catches you. Can you imagine what those kids think about us? They'll think we're from the funny farm!"

Joe shrugged his shoulders. "Maybe I am!"

When we got to *Corazón*, Cory was sitting on a boulder taking a bath, her leg stretched forth as she licked her paws. She stood up for our approach.

"I'll catch her a fish after a while," I said, and we began to unload all our purchases on the boulder.

"I'm pouring a cement landing on this today," Joe commented, "so it won't be so hard to get in and out of the boat. And I'll fix us some kind of steps beside the coconut tree so we don't fall with all our supplies on the way up to the campsite."

"Great!" I looked forward to improvements.

Mercedes and Leonso jumped down the rocks to help us. In a few minutes we had the supplies unloaded and carried up to the upper level of the island.

One boulder the size of our truck was resting precariously against one of the house jacks.

Joe patted the men on the back and congratulated them on how well they had done since we had left. I couldn't really see that they had done so much, but I wasn't going to comment.

Joe hurried into the tent and changed into his old faded gym shorts and ran to the lake to jump in. As he came up out of the water, he shouted, "Sandy, come on. You'll feel so much better."

I was still a bit wary of just jumping in anywhere. The stories of freshwater sharks still haunted me and I didn't want to swim where I wasn't protected by rocks or something. On Tomme Terre, we had had several huge boulders that made a safe enclosure for swimming, bathing, and washing clothes, but I hadn't seen a similar safe area on this island.

"I'll put up the groceries first and then, maybe," I answered.

Joe climbed up the smooth black rocks and shook his hair dry. He called for the two men to join him where the boat was parked. He got a steel tool called a star drill and began to pound the boulder with a sledge hammer. Then he let Leonso try it.

I walked over to see what was going on. "I'm putting two anchor bolts in the rock so we can hang tires from this boulder and park the boat here," Joe explained. "Then, we'll pour a layer of cement on top for a flat dock."

One end of the boulder had a flat incline going down into the water. "Hey, Joe," I called, "look at this end of the boulder. Looks like a perfect spot for me to wash clothes."

He jumped down into the water and inspected the boulder. "You're right," he said, "I'll fix you a place to stand right here and a log going across so the clothes won't wash away before you rinse them."

As I stood there staring at the new "laundry room," Cory brushed against my legs. I bent over and patted her. "What's happening to your world, little one?" I asked aloud and privately wondered about my own.

The Wilsons had loaned us a hibachi grill, so I went around the island gathering up firewood to boil a day's supply of water. I carried the copper kettle we had received as a wedding gift down to the lake and filled it up. We had two collapsible plastic gallon containers for storing our purified water. Once I got the fire going, it took about forty-five minutes to fill the containers with water.

After that was done, I decided to wash the few clothes we had soiled so the laundry wouldn't pile up. Washing was such a job I had to do it every day. My arms were so tired by the time I finished rinsing, I wondered if I would ever be "in shape" for the chore.

I called for Joe to carry the big green tub of clean clothes out to the other end of the island. After hanging them out to dry, it was time to prepare our lunch.

I could see the men stacking rocks beneath a coconut tree. They were building the steps up from the water. The three of them talked and laughed as they worked. I suddenly felt very lonely. Cory scampered by as if to tease me into a chase.

I went to the shelter we called our kitchen and got the bag of meat out of the cooler. I took the new grinder from the box and hooked it to the plywood cupboard. As I ground the meat, I was surprised that there was no fat in it. It was solid dark red throughout with not even one streak of white.

I finally got enough ground up for three burgers. Joe would be hungry, and I was in the mood for a good hamburger myself.

The hibachi still had some hot coals from boiling the water, so I added some more branches to make the fire hotter. When the coals were glowing, I put on the burgers.

Suddenly, Joe was standing above me. "Smells great!" he said sniffing the air. "When will it be ready?"

I said I wasn't sure and he went on back to work. I looked toward the mouth of the channel at Mercedes' island and saw a tiny dugout on its way. *That will be one of the children with their daddy's lunch,* I thought, and bent over to check on ours.

One of Leonso's younger sons brought his. The young boy came up to the top of the island and stared at me. He was grinning just as Mario had done when I first met him. He stuck up his hand and said, "Hola."

I asked him his name and he rattled off something followed by "Happy Uncle." Len had told us about him, the young boy who was always happy. The Wilsons had nicknamed him Happy Uncle and it had stuck. I shook his hand and he looked curiously at what I was cooking.

I said, "Hamburger?"

His eyes lit up with recognition. "Oh, *sí*, like Señor Wilson?"

I nodded and heard his dad calling for him. He said good-by and left.

Joe and I ate, holding our camp plates on our knees. "Think we could buy a table and chairs or something?" I asked. My back was so tired.

"I don't know," Joe answered. His thoughts were elsewhere as he talked of the work that needed to be done. He finished quickly and kissed me on the cheek before going back to his project.

I filled the washtub with hot, sudsy water and washed the plates and cups. As I tossed the dishwater into the lake, hundreds of fish bobbed to the surface for the food particles in the suds.

I grabbed our bamboo pole, put a piece of bread on the hook, and tossed it in. As soon as the morsel hit the water, a six-inch silver fish bit the hook! "Joe," I screamed, "come quick."

I could hear Joe above me. "Where are you?" he shouted in a panic-stricken voice.

"I'm okay," I shouted back, realizing he thought something was wrong. "Look," I said proudly as he looked down at me. I held the shiny fish in the air.

Mercedes and Leonso stared from behind him and laughed. Mercedes joined me at the water's edge and explained that he would show me some real fishing when he finished working.

After sitting for hours just to catch blue gill at home in Tennessee, I had caught a bigger fish in less than a minute here.

I took the fish up to Cory. It was still alive as she pounced on it. *At least she appreciates my efforts*, I thought.

Instead of going home at 2:30, as they were supposed to, the men continued working on the huge boulder. We realized it was going to take days to move each one, and the rainy season was approaching.

The three men began struggling with the boulder. It moved a foot that afternoon.

"At this rate," I said, "we'll be in the tent forever."

Leonso suggested to Joe that they use both jacks and see if they could make more progress. They finally found a place to hook the other jack and used the steel bar to crank the boulder up a few inches. Joe yelled for me to bring some rocks to put under the huge boulder so it wouldn't fall back down. I found a perfect-size rock and struggled to carry it to them.

It was 4:30 when the men insisted they must go home. I felt relieved. Now maybe Joe and I could have some privacy and talk.

I was wrong! He had allowed the men to quit working, but he still worked on, struggling with the huge boulder alone and screaming at me to carry rock.

About 5:30 he asked me what I planned for supper because he was getting really hungry. I just glared at him. My hands were raw from the rocks; I still had to bring in the laundry; I was sweaty and dirty; and I certainly didn't feel like cooking.

I stomped into the "kitchen" and looked in the cooler again. Eggs! Surely an omelet would be quick and easy.

I got out the Coleman stove and pumped it up. I didn't care if I used all the fuel. It was faster than building another fire.

I cut up a salad and we were soon crouching on a rock eating again. I felt that was all I'd done all day—cook and eat.

After supper and cleaning up the dishes, I sat down on a rock and stared at the water. The sun had dropped behind Mombacho in a glorious blaze of pink and orange. Joe was checking the new anchor bolts on the docking rock.

"How can I bathe?" I called down to him.

"Just jump in," he said.

"I can't do that!" I insisted. "How will I get clean? I want to take a real bath—with soap and a washcloth!"

Joe glanced at my washing rock. "Why don't you just sit on your platform rock and I'll keep watch for you."

"Can't we put up a sheet or something?" I felt so tired, but I just couldn't go to bed dirty.

"Oh, come on, Sandy," Joe insisted. "Nobody is looking anyway."

The steps they'd built that day were handy. I carefully stepped down to the dock level and got in the cool water. After being so hot all day, I thought the water felt cold but it must have been at least sixty degrees.

A Christmas wedding. We exchanged vows December 27, 1975.

My bamboo-framed, tarp-covered kitchen the day after we bought the new gas oven. This was my first pan of cornbread in three months.

Cory watches as I clean a fish.

The wash rock where I lost my ring.

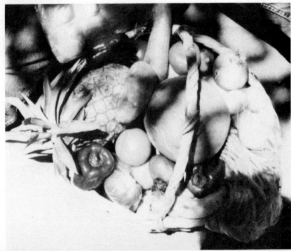

One week's groceries—$2.50.

Mercedes and his family in front of their home. Pictured right to left: Mercedes, Rosa Elena holding her new baby Luisa, Carlita, Maria, Teresa, Rosita, Marta holding her new baby, Enrique, and Mercedes, Jr.

Joe and Mercedes planing the mahogany beams. "Better get a hat on," Mercedes warned. Joe learned the hard way.

Raising the roof beams.

Applying paint to Joe's
screened, acrylic-coated roof.

The finished roof with diamond-shaped skylight and mahogany trim. Its
unique design trapped and ventilated heat away from the house.

Our home! Now with the louvers open and the trees in full foliage—beautiful!

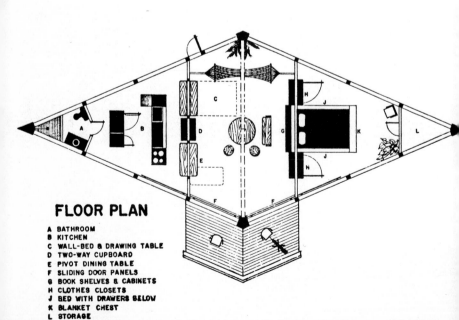

FLOOR PLAN

A BATHROOM
B KITCHEN
C WALL-BED & DRAWING TABLE
D TWO-WAY CUPBOARD
E PIVOT DINING TABLE
F SLIDING DOOR PANELS
G BOOK SHELVES & CABINETS
H CLOTHES CLOSETS
J BED WITH DRAWERS BELOW
K BLANKET CHEST
L STORAGE

A closeup view of the house.

The interior of the living area. Joe's mom is at the table showing one of our catches from the lake and his stepfather is in the hammock.

Two views of El Corazón. In the aerial photo, our island is in the
heart of the channel. Mercedes' island is to the right and Zapatera,
the boot-shaped island, is to the left.

As I took my clothes off, it seemed to me there were eyes peeking from everywhere in the lake. I also worried about all those fish in the water.

Joe stood guard while I soaped up and rinsed. I put on my bathrobe and headed back toward the tent. I did feel better.

"You'll get used to it after a while," Joe said encouragingly.

I didn't answer. I was beginning to wonder if I would ever get used to this primitive life. As I went to sleep, I thought of my mom's cooking and a wonderful bathtub.

The next morning I felt rested and determined to have a better attitude. It was Sunday. The men had said they didn't want to work on this day, and I hoped Joe and I could rest and talk.

I missed talking. For the past year, we had talked incessantly of our plans to be here. Now that we were here, we didn't seem to talk much at all.

As I sat near the dock, Cory hopped up from the rocks. She was still sleeping in her little cave. Joe and I had decided to make a rock patio in that area of the island and I hoped she would soon find another place to sleep.

It was a sparkling day. I walked out to the end of the island and looked toward the open water. A dugout with a sail was just barely visible far away. I looked forward to the time when we could enjoy our surroundings instead of constantly working.

Joe was calling for me and I went back to the tent. "What are you doing?" he asked sleepily.

"Just walking around."

"Why don't you come to bed?"

I unzipped the tent and Cory ran inside. She nuzzled against Joe, begging to be petted.

"Well, now," I said, "isn't she the spoiled one? I won't worry about her from now on. That cat can take care of herself."

I crawled back into bed beside Joe, and she stepped cautiously over him and lay between us. Her loud purring convinced us we had a contented cat.

"Are you hungry?" I asked, hoping the answer was no. I just didn't want to spend the whole day cooking.

"No," Joe answered, "in fact, I think maybe it would be better for us both if you just fixed two meals a day. Since we can make our own schedule, why don't we eat in the midmorning and then again in the late afternoon?"

"Sounds great to me!" I quickly agreed. A tremendous weight had just been lifted off me. How did our grandmothers ever do it? Especially with lots of children to feed? And the weather wasn't even warm several months of the year! I just couldn't imagine it.

We were both just beginning to understand what it had taken for people to settle in our homeland—and to question what had made our country so different. Why was it that so many people we'd met in Nicaragua still lived as they had a century ago? We couldn't figure out the answers.

"Let's go visit the Wilsons," Joe said after we'd eaten our late morning breakfast. "They've been so nice to us."

We went down to get in the boat. As we sped across the water, we heard a knocking noise coming from the motor.

"Oh, no!" I cried. "That's all we need."

Joe stopped the engine and took the top off the motor. "I can't see anything wrong."

As we started out again, the noise was the same. "Could we be hitting rocks or something?" I asked.

"No," Joe replied, "I don't think so. Maybe Len will have an idea of what it is."

After riding around with us for a few minutes, Len suggested we see the mechanic in Granada. "You never know. He could be at the dock working on another boat. I see him there a lot."

We thanked him and headed back to our island. "At least we have the little five-horse motor if we need it," Joe said, "but it would be so slow I don't want to use it if we can get this one fixed."

We got back to the island in time to watch the sunset and wished we could share all its beauty with our families. It had been a week since we'd gotten any mail and I was getting more and more homesick.

On Monday morning, the men showed up at 6:30 sharp and immediately went to work trying to move the huge boulder in the middle of the island.

Joe and I went into town to find the mechanic, a black man from the east coast who spoke an interesting mixture of Spanish and pirate-English. He was very friendly and insisted we call him by his nickname, "Chicken."

He and his family lived in a little shack on a dirt road just three blocks from the post office. Motor parts were lying everywhere. A water barrel stood outside the front door. He and Joe attached our motor to the side of the barrel and cranked it.

Water churned over the sides of the barrel, and the motor began to knock as it had done on the lake. Chicken stood there biting his lip and shaking his head. After a few minutes, he turned off the motor. Joe and I looked at him expectantly.

"Jyes, ze problem kin be mended," he said with his strange blend of languages. "Kin ye come back in 'alf hour?"

"Yes, yes," we said, patting him on the back and shaking his hand.

We drove to the post office and I ran in. I almost dreaded to look in the window of our shiny brass box, numbered 238. *Mail!* I was so excited I could hardly work the combination. There were a cassette tape message from my dad, a letter from Joe's mom, and two other letters from friends.

I skipped joyously out to where Joe was waiting, hiding our bounty behind my back to surprise him.

"No need to hide whatever it is," he said. "From the look on your face I know we got mail."

I jumped in the truck beside him and began to tear open the letters. "Oh, I wish we had brought the tape player so I could hear this one," I said impatiently.

"It'll be something to look forward to when we get back to the island."

We devoured every word of the letters. It was so good to hear from home and know everyone was okay.

When the familiar sound of the ice cream vendor's tinkling bells filled the air, Joe offered, "How about a creamsicle?"

"Why not?" I answered.

So we sat there reading letters and slurping the sticky orange and vanilla ice cream as people walked around the truck staring at the gringos.

We went back to Chicken's house after a while, and he showed us the worn gear he had replaced. We paid him and loaded the heavy motor back into the truck.

"You want to take some of the clothes and the trunk out to the island today?" Joe asked as we bumped down the dusty road to the dock.

"Oh, yes," I replied. "I wish we could unload the two crates, too. I worry about our china. I hope these bumpy roads haven't broken it all to pieces."

"We can't take it all in one load," Joe reminded me. "Every time we come into town, we'll haul something else out, okay?"

"Okay," I said and reached over to hug him.

I felt so happy. I couldn't wait to get to the island so I could listen to Dad's tape.

Joe strained and grunted as he lowered the heavy motor, trunk, and piles of clothes into the boat. Then he took off his shirt and sandals and we skimmed across the water.

As we approached the island we could see little Cory on the rocks. She evidently recognized the sound of our motor now and was always waiting.

"Hi, little one," I said as we tied the boat to the newly placed anchor bolts. She rubbed against me and purred loudly.

We carried everything on up to the tent. "These steps sure are better," I complimented Joe. "Every little improvement helps."

We looked up and stopped in our tracks. Mercedes and Leonso were straining with all their might as they pushed down on the steel bar, cranking up the house jack under the huge boulder. It had actually moved while we were gone!

Joe set the trunk down in the dirt and ran to help. Suddenly there was a loud snap and the boulder rested back down on the pile of rocks beneath it. The men jumped back, stumbling.

"What happened?" I cried, running over to see if any of them was hurt.

Leonso was inspecting one of the jacks. It had broken from the weight.

"Can it be repaired?" I asked Joe.

"Oh, we can probably find someone to weld it back," he answered optimistically.

Assured that no one was hurt, I went to the tent to change into my cut-offs and top, fix a good lunch, and rearrange the tent with our trunk under one window. Our tent was beginning to look like a cozy little cottage, a perfect place for me to relax and enjoy Dad's tape.

Later I sat down to write letters and add some notes in my diary:

Today was the first day I've actually realized how fortunate we are to have such a place and the time, energy, knowledge, and money to do something with it. Sure, I get homesick, but writing letters today helped a whole lot. I kept thinking of other people's lives—their problems and disregarded dreams. Joe and I have truly been blessed. Oh, dearest God, show us your way.

The next morning we had to go to Managua. After leaving the jack to be welded at a shop in Masaya, we drove on to the American Embassy to register our marriage certificate and get my passport name changed to my married name.

Then we went to several stores that sold kerosene refrigerators. I really hoped we could get one soon, but every one we looked at cost much more than we wanted to pay. I was discouraged but Joe assured me we would find one soon.

In the meantime, I was looking at the propane gas stoves. I also looked forward to the time I wouldn't have to build fires for cooking.

We stopped by the residence for University of Tennessee architecture students. Some of the students gave us books, and I looked forward to reading the latest best-sellers.

We made a final stop at the fancy supermarket as we left town. The difference in prices from what I'd been paying in the Granada market was shocking. No wonder Joe wanted me to shop there. The few canned goods I bought cost five times what they would in the U.S.

For a few cordobas the jack was welded and better than new with the stronger support.

By dusk we were back on the island. Mercedes and Leonso had stacked rock all day and were well on the way to completing our patio above Cory's cave. The beautiful rock work, done without mortar, had brought our dream nearer to realization. It had been a good day.

The next few days flew by in a daily routine with occasional trips to town for supplies and groceries. By Valentine's Day we were falling in love with our little island named The Heart.

That Saturday dawned bright and clear. Joe was acting strangely, as if he had a secret. About ten o'clock he suggested that I walk out to the other end of the island and look at the beautiful orchids growing on the rocks.

"Why?" I asked. "Have they changed any since yesterday?"

"No," he replied. "Just go see."

I walked out to the clothesline and looked at the dainty little flowers. I could see nothing different about them. Then, as I turned around, I saw it. Permanently carved on the side of a huge boulder was a three-foot heart with our initials inside it!

Joe stepped from behind the rock to see my reaction. "Happy Valentine's Day, sweetheart."

"But, but," I stammered, "when did you do this?"

"I sneaked out of bed and used a sharp rock to carve the surface. I was always afraid you'd wake up and catch me, but you didn't."

I walked over to him and hugged his neck. "I love you so much."

We leaned against the heart and looked out at the open lake. This really was our very own island.

TEN

Except the Lord Build a House

The next few days were full of progress. Hours of nonstop work finally brought the boulder to the edge of the island. With one final push, it tumbled off and thundered into the lake. At last one mountain was moved. Only two more to go.

Each night, we collapsed into bed and wondered if we could ever get up again. *How can paradise be so much work?* I would wonder as I fell into deep sleep.

After three weeks, the last of the boulders was buried in a huge hole, and the leveled area on top of the island was ready for staking out the house.

"Let's go on and buy our stove now," I pleaded with Joe. "We'll be in the house before long."

"Whoa!" he said. "Hold your horses. We're just now beginning the hard part."

He was busy measuring and cutting sticks to stake out the foundation of the house. The men were building a rock retaining wall around the fruit trees on the back of the island. Since the wall had to be a solid layer of rock held with mortar, it was a new kind of project for them, and they were leaving unsightly cement cakes on the stones.

After cooking, hauling, and boiling our drinking water and cleaning the tent, I stood watching them sling the mortar into place like two preschoolers slinging mud. I couldn't stand the mess any longer.

"Joe," I called, "would you look at that mess? We don't want that wall to look like that, do we?"

Joe looked at it and shook his head. "They're sure not used to working with cement."

He went over and started helping them. I noticed the sticks and string he had left lying on the ground. He shouldn't have to waste his time working on a wall. Maybe I could help the men. After all, I had often watched my uncle lay bricks.

Three days and five pairs of gloves later, the wall was complete and beautiful. Mercedes and Leonso just stood and stared at me, a woman who could do this kind of work. Joe took pictures of the job and kept on congratulating me.

I felt really proud, even if my hands and fingertips were raw. Up to that time, the tasks I had been doing were so repetitive. Now, I felt I had really helped build our dream.

Joe had been right about the work's just beginning. Some days, I had to beg him to take time off to eat. He was up and working each morning before Mercedes came to work, and he drove himself like a mule until long after dark.

We hauled lumber, forty bags of cement, sixty sacks of sand, and endless little supplies like nails and string.

Joe let Leonso stop working because it was so hard to explain to both men everything that had to be done. He decided he'd rather do the backbreaking work himself with only Mercedes as a helper.

One afternoon as I carried the sheets and our clothes down to the lake to wash, I stepped down into the water and looked back toward the men as they worked. Joe laughed with Mercedes as they built the last of the forms for the support columns of the house. I felt so left out.

As I sprinkled the detergent on Joe's jeans, I began to wonder what kind of life I'd gotten myself into. I pounded the clothes into the rock and replayed the last few days in my mind.

Up at dawn to begin the daily chores of carrying water, building a fire, boiling, cooking, planning one difficult meal after another with our limited facilities, dumping the potty, cleaning the tent, keeping the dirt floor swept clean and sprinkled with water so our tent would remain clean, doing the laundry, hauling, loading, unloading, on and on. Then, Joe expected me to be his lover as he fell into bed at night after hardly a full sentence of conversation all day. *I just can't go on*, I thought.

Suddenly, I looked down at my soapy hands. My wedding band was missing from my finger. Tears filled my eyes. Where could it be? I had promised myself before we were married that it would never come off my finger for the rest of my life.

"Joe!" I screamed. "Come quick!"

"What's the matter?!!" he shouted as he half-fell down the steps. "Did you see a shark?"

"No," I sobbed. "My wedding band—it's gone!"

"What were you doing with it on?" Joe asked incredulously. "Don't you take it off when you're washing clothes?"

"Don't you even remember?" I screamed at him.

"Remember what?"

"I swore I'd never take it off. It's your fault. It wouldn't have happened if you hadn't brought me here."

I stomped up the steps, jerked the zipper open on the tent, and fell down on the bed. Mercedes stood staring at me through the screen, with a puzzled look on his face. He couldn't figure out what in the world was going on.

"*Amigo*," Joe called, "*ayúdame, por favor*."

After a while I got up and looked down at the laundry rock. Joe and Mercedes were taking turns diving among the rocks to search for the tiny band of gold.

I couldn't stop crying. The ring meant so much to me. We had designed the matched set ourselves, and they had been handmade just for us. Mine could never be replaced.

It was getting dark when Joe came to the tent opening. I turned over. "Did you find it?" I asked hopefully.

He shook his head sadly, and I began to cry again. "I just want to go home. Please let me go home."

Joe knelt beside me and jerked my arm. He glared into my eyes. "Do you mean to tell me," he said angrily, "you care more for that stupid ring than me?"

"No," I sobbed, but I wasn't really sure.

"If it means that much to you, then I'll ask God almighty to help me find it!"

I couldn't imagine any possible way the ring would ever be found in all the rocks around the laundry area. The men had moved most of the smaller ones already, and now I didn't have a sheltered place to bathe either.

I cried myself to sleep that night. Joe hugged his side of the bed and I hugged against the canvas wall of the tent. It was the first night we had gone to sleep angry with each other.

The next morning dawned as usual. My hand felt naked without the ring on my finger. Joe was already out of bed when I got up. He and Mercedes were maneuvering the heavy house jack down in the water.

"What are you trying to do now?" I asked cautiously.

Joe got out of the water and bounded up the steps. "Sandy," he said, putting his hands on my shoulders and gently squeezing, "I know we've always thought that God is only interested in big things, but this morning I remembered meeting Andy in Mexico and how we found that village in the mountains and had his car repaired. Well, I think we ought to pray and really expect God to answer, okay?"

I didn't answer but looked up into the sky. I didn't know if I could believe it or not. Joe spoke aloud, "God, you know how much this ring means to Sandy. Please help me find it for her. In Jesus' name, amen."

He jumped back down the steps and into the water. He and Mercedes placed the jack on the huge flat rock I had used as a laundry platform. They heaved and pushed until it rolled into the water. I could imagine the ring being lost forever or smashed to pieces by all the rocks.

The water turned muddy from all the activity. When it finally cleared, Joe cheered. "There it is!"

I ran to the rock and stared down into the water. There, in the center of a huge boulder was the glistening band of gold!

"Can you believe it?" Joe exclaimed as he put the ring on my finger and kissed me. We both suddenly realized we had a lot to learn about expanding our narrow concept of God. He might help us understand each other.

As I fixed our morning meal, I watched Joe pour the last bucket of cement into the eight-foot form for the column to support the roof beams of our house. He patiently worked with the steel saddle that would extend out of the hardened cement. He was trying to be sure every detail was perfect.

After breakfast, I began unpacking the trunk of books we had brought out a couple of days before. The crate contained some of my favorites, and I saw the gift box containing a Bible I'd been given for graduation. I opened it and flipped through it. Suddenly a verse caught my eye: "Except the Lord build a house, they labor in vain who build it."

I looked out at Joe's handiwork and thought for a long time. How *does* the Lord build a house?

ELEVEN

Doubts + Delays = Discouragement

On the morning of February 27, I glanced at the calendar. It was our two-month anniversary. *How could two months pass so quickly?* I wondered.

"Sandy," Joe called from where he and Mercedes were building a stone wall for what would soon be our bedroom, "we're going into town in an hour or so. Better make a list of anything you need."

Joe hadn't mentioned anything about a trip to town for today. While I finished dressing and listed the groceries, I wondered what we needed that couldn't wait until tomorrow, our regular market day.

Mercedes stayed and worked on the wall while we sped across the water toward Asese. "How come you decided to go in today?" I asked.

"Oh, didn't I tell you? We get to pick out a mahogany tree for the beams of our house!"

It was time for some real progress. The footings had been poured and Joe had ripped off the forms the afternoon before.

"I hope I can find the sawmill," Joe said as we loaded the cooler and gas tank in the truck.

We turned down a one-lane, tree-lined road and the air felt cooler. Huge oxen teams were dragging bigger logs than I had ever seen.

We stopped beside a pile of three- to four-foot diameter logs. The saw mill, a rambling collection of wood-framed buildings covered with tin roofing, had obviously grown with the business over the years.

I got out of the truck and sat on top of one of the huge, freshly cut mahogany trees while Joe talked with the owner about our needs.

In a little while he walked toward me and motioned for me to follow him. We stood inside the shelter and watched several barefoot men feed huge logs through a stripper that removed the bark, then carry them across to a huge, whirring saw that squared up the logs.

"We'll pick out a tree, and they'll cut it up any way we want it," Joe shouted above the noise of the saw.

I nodded my head with interest. We watched the men work for a little while and then walked out into the sunlight to inspect the trees that lay neatly beside the driveway. "We pay for the whole tree and get every part we can haul off."

"At least I'll have plenty of firewood now," I commented, looking at the bark of the twenty foot log.

We finally decided which tree we would buy and with the owner's advice were assured it could be cut to meet our needs by the first of the week.

We hopped into the truck like two excited children. Talking excitedly about the house, Joe turned on the ignition and began backing up. Suddenly, we felt a jolt and I looked out my window. The right rear fender was mashed against the end of a log.

"Oh, no," I moaned, "look what you've done!"

He jumped out and ran around to look. "It'll pop back out," he said with confidence.

But as we pulled up, the dent stayed in the metal. I felt sick. Our pretty truck was now flawed, and it was Joe's fault. *If he hadn't been talking, it wouldn't have happened,* I thought smugly.

"Nothing we can do about it now," he said as we drove back down the tree-lined lane. "We'll just have to work on it some other time."

We took a different road toward town. On my left was a beautiful cemetery. Huge tombs and statues sparkled in the glaring sun.

"We've never been this way before." I stared at the beautiful entrance.

"No," Joe agreed, "we're going to a new store."

"What kind of store?" I asked, but he just shrugged his shoulders and looked at me mischievously.

Now my curiosity was piqued, but I didn't have long to wait. We stopped in front of an appliance store, and I was afraid to guess why.

"It's our second anniversary," Joe reminded me, "and we're buying you a new stove!"

I jumped up and down and hugged him as we entered the store. The owner and his family sat around in rocking chairs, and he stood as we entered.

I spotted a shiny yellow-enameled stove with four burners and a large oven. *"Cuánto cuesta?"* I asked, hoping the price was what we had planned to spend. The price was higher than we expected and I told him so. Joe sat down and watched me curiously. He had not seen me use my newly acquired bartering skill.

The owner brought the price down a little, but I still wasn't satisfied that he was giving me a fair price. I asked him if he understood that I am now a Nicaraguan and expected to be treated as one of his neighbors.

"No *soy* una tourista," I assured him. He threw up his hands in defeat, and we met a fair compromise.

Joe stood up. "You sure have learned the system!" he congratulated me. "I see now what the market taught you."

The owner's family helped Joe load our beautiful new gas stove into the back of the camper. As Joe scooted into the driver's seat, I attacked him with hugs and kisses. "What an anniversary!" I squealed. "Lumber for you and a stove for me. Let's do this every month!"

"That's a great idea," Joe laughed.

Mercedes met us at the dock on our island. He admired the stove as much as I did and helped Joe carry it to the shelter. They placed it on the hard-packed earth beside our pantry, and I sat down to figure out how to operate it. We had purchased a tank of "Tropigas" to go with it, and I also wondered how long the fuel would last. I'd never used gas before and I didn't want to mess anything up.

Meanwhile Joe slipped on his old, faded orange gym shorts and went to work on the wall with Mercedes.

My mouth watered as I lit the oven for the first time. I had bought some freshly ground cornmeal in the market and was determined to have my first taste of real Tennessee cornbread in more than two months.

Just forty-five minutes later, I took the black skillet from the oven and shouted for Joe. "Get the camera," I screamed. "I want this recorded for history."

His mouth dropped open when he saw the steaming bread, "Oh,

gosh," he admitted, "I'd forgotten about all the good things that come from ovens!"

We cut the cornbread into three huge pieces and shared the mouth-watering delicacy with Mercedes. He agreed he'd never tasted cornbread like that before and hoped I would make some for his family.

That night I wrote in my diary, *I think we're over the hump—from worse to better!* Little did I know what lay ahead.

My happiness over the stove was short-lived. In the coming days, all Joe thought about was the house. For more than a year, he had systematically built it in his imagination over and over. Now that it was actually happening, he could think of nothing else. I began to feel so lonely for someone to talk with. I longed to go home.

The mahogany beams were indeed beautiful. We made two trips into Granada hauling the twenty-foot beams on the boat trailer. It took three men to load and unload them into a huge dugout we had rented for the day.

Joe talked a mile a minute as he swerved along the narrow roads to the sawmill. "Do you realize those beams are actually oversized? I ordered six-by-six inches and these are seven and a half to eight inches square! Nobody in the States would believe this kind of lumber. It's fantastic. I can just see them in place now."

When we brought the last load to Asese, we discovered one beam was missing. Joe kept figuring and refiguring, but it always came out the same—one short. He hopped in the truck, leaving me standing at the dock as he sped off back toward town. Fifteen minutes later he was back with the lone beam tied on the trailer behind him.

"It had fallen off in a barrio near the saw mill," he panted as he and Len placed it with the others in the dugout. "I'm so glad it was still there. Someone could have taken it."

Mercedes was on *Corazón* when we arrived. The dugout followed slowly behind us with its heavy load. He had already helped unload the first load, and the golden beams lay across a huge boulder waiting to be carried to the upper part of the island.

Joe called happily to him and parked the boat out of the way. "Sandy, get some lunch ready, will you?" he commanded. "We've got a lot to do today."

I don't know whether it was the tone of his voice or the fact he'd just left me standing there at Asese in his excitement about the lost beam, or a combination of everything, but I suddenly had the idea that I had been relegated to a slave position. He didn't even boss Mercedes around in that tone of voice.

I tried not to let the hurt show as I went through the motions of fixing our lunch, but I couldn't help noticing Joe's camaraderie with Mercedes as they struggled with each beam.

They finally had the beams stacked neatly in front of the tent in the shade of a coconut tree. Joe stooped over and caressed each beam.

"Aren't they beautiful?" he asked with awe, "It's got to be the most beautiful lumber in the world. Nothing could top Honduran mahogany for this house—nothing."

I winced at his words. It had been several weeks since he'd spoken to me that tenderly. I had the feeling he was in love with this inanimate object and had forgotten about me.

"You're jealous of this whole project," I heard an inner voice say. I pushed at the meat cooking in the skillet. *I've got a right to be*, I wanted to scream.

Joe sat down, said a prayer over the food, and thanked God for the beautiful lumber. He mechanically pecked me on the lips and talked all through the meal about how strong the house would be, what fun it would be to show it all off to our families.

"After all, this house will be one of a kind with all these beautiful materials," he stated proudly.

In just moments he had finished eating and jumped up to resume working. He was doing last-minute cleaning of the tall concrete columns that would be the main supports of the roof beams. I could see him running the palms of his hands over each side and corner, sanding any little flaw from the surface of each one.

Len had loaned Joe his plane, and Mercedes had two ancient-looking hand planes of his own. The rough, sawn surface wasn't good enough for Joe, and they began the tedious job of planing the long beams by hand. Joe stroked each beam reverently and slowly began to plane away the rough edges.

I felt more and more left out. After hanging out the laundry that afternoon I went into the tent and got out our wedding scrapbook. I looked wistfully at our pictures. Just two and a half months earlier my hair was fixed just so—every strand in place. Joe held my eyes with the same look I had seen him use on those stupid beams! I slammed the book closed.

"How can I be jealous of lumber and an illiterate native?" my mind screamed.

Then I heard familiar voices. The Wilsons had come to see our latest purchase. The interruption made me even angrier.

Bea had brought a cooler of ice and water. With her diabetes she was always thirsty. She panted up the steps, and Len opened the lawn chair they had brought for her.

"Well," she sat and snorted for breath, "looks like it's shaping up around here."

"I guess so," I replied half-heartedly.

"What's the matter?" she asked. "Homesick?"

"I guess so," I answered again. I wasn't going to tell her what was really wrong. It wasn't her business.

After about ten minutes she began to complain to Len that she must go back home and get in bed. The dust and particles from the shavings were irritating her emphysema, and she was having trouble breathing.

He reluctantly packed her and the chair into their fiber-glass boat, and Leonso drove them slowly out of sight. They never ventured off their regular route without him because they feared more than anything the possibility of damaging the boat on the submerged rocks throughout the lake.

I waved good-by until they were out of sight. Cory lay on the rock next to me. "Oh, Cory, what are we to do?" I asked her. She purred loudly as I petted her and grew more and more depressed.

That evening Joe took his customary jump in the lake to clean up. His back was dark reddish-brown from his days in the scorching sun. He was a beautiful man. In spite of my anger and my jealous thoughts, I still loved him. I watched him bathe and feared he had lost those feelings about me.

Before we were married, I had always had time to roll my hair, get my makeup just right, and dress just so. Now, I couldn't even see myself in the tiny makeup mirror we had. I certainly couldn't fix my hair the way I'd always worn it—not without electricity. Even if I could have, the wind on the island would have blown it straight the next minute.

Joe let out his nightly Tarzan yell and bounded up the steps to the tent.

"You should try to get used to the water," he encouraged me. "There aren't any sharks this close in."

"I will soon," I said unconvincingly.

We got into bed and Joe began talking about the house again. I went to sleep as he was describing some kind of old tool Mercedes was going to bring to cut the beams with.

The next day, I woke up determined to do something special so I would feel a little more useful. First I decided to make something different for breakfast, something Joe would really enjoy and appreciate for a change.

I'd never made hash browns before, but I knew it was one of Joe's favorites. I hurriedly pulled on my cut-offs and top, brushed back my hair into a clasp, and went out to the kitchen.

I picked out some smooth potatoes and peeled them. Then I started grating them and hoped I was doing it correctly. I poured cooking oil into the skillet and let it get hot. But when I put the first handful into the skillet, they just sat there in the grease. The wind was blowing the flame sideways. I set the cooler up on the plywood cupboard beside the stove and blocked the wind a little.

In the meantime, I fixed eggs, toast, fruit, and cereal. The hash browns seemed to be cooking, but certainly didn't look like any hash browns I'd ever seen. They were soggy with grease and didn't turn very brown at all. I was getting frustrated with the whole process when Joe yelled from the middle of the island, "Isn't breakfast ready yet? I'm starved."

I plopped the potato mess onto a paper towel and tried my best to absorb some of the grease. Joe came around the corner of our bamboo-framed hut and asked again, "Is it ready?"

"Yeah," I half-screamed. "Sit down and eat it!" I was just about ready to cry. Even when I tried to do something special, I messed it up.

"What's the matter with you?"

"Nothing!"

"Well there's got to be something," he said as we sat down. He grabbed my hand, said the blessing, pecked me on the lips, and began to eat.

I watched closely as he took a bite of the hash browns. He stopped chewing. "What is this?" he asked.

"It's awful, isn't it?"

"Not too bad, but what is it?"

"It was supposed to be hash browns," I said tearfully, "but admit it, they're terrible, aren't they?"

"No!" Joe insisted. "Now, don't start crying over something so silly."

"It's not silly," I insisted. "I tried so hard to cook something special for you and I only made a mess!"

"What are you talking about?" Joe demanded. "Who cares about hash browns anyway?"

"I do!"

"Well," Joe threatened, "if you keep on making such a big deal about them, I'm tossing the whole meal into the lake. It's not worth this kind of arguing!"

"But you don't understand," I cried. "I wanted to . . ."

Suddenly, Joe jumped up with the plates and slung the contents out into the water. I jumped up to try to stop him, but hundreds of fish were already enjoying our breakfast. That was it!

I stomped into the tent and began throwing some clothes and my makeup into a suitcase. I grabbed our bankbook and my passport. Joe came to the open tent and looked in.

"What do you think you're doing?" he asked hatefully.

I just kept packing and refused to answer. I wasn't going to speak to such an insensitive ogre.

I finally had everything I thought I needed and flung back the zippered opening of the tent and marched down to the boat. Joe stood under the coconut tree watching in bewilderment. I could see Mercedes planing a log as fast as he could, carefully not looking in our direction.

I jumped into the boat and walked to the back. Tears were stinging my eyes and rolling down my cheeks. I grabbed for the rope and began to jerk at the motor. The boat rocked in the water as I tried repeatedly to get the motor to crank.

Out of the corner of my eye I saw Joe sitting on the top step beneath the coconut tree, watching. I was more determined than ever and I grabbed the rope one last time to start the motor. "You don't care about me any more," I screamed. "All you care about is this dumb island, your fancy house, and proving to the world what a good designer you are! You don't need me!"

Suddenly, the boat rocked and I started falling. I tried to grab the side to get my balance, but I was overboard before I could even catch my breath. I fought to the surface of the water, imagining the sharks closing in around me as I scrambled up some rocks.

Joe came running down the steps. I lay on a boulder, dripping with water, panting to catch my breath.

"Is that what you really think?" Joe asked cautiously as he came to sit beside me. "Do you really think all I care about is this island?"

"It's true," I said starting to cry again. "You don't even talk to me any-more. You don't notice whether I'm alive or dead except when you're hungry or ready for bed!"

Joe stared at me and didn't say a word. He was thinking before he spoke. I felt better than I had in days. It felt good finally saying every-thing I'd been thinking. I didn't care what he thought about me, I just had to tell him how I felt.

After a few minutes of silence, Joe looked into my eyes. I didn't want to look at him, but he begged me to.

"Sandy," he spoke, "I'm so sorry. You're exactly right. I've been so ex-cited about the house and all our dreams coming true that I forgot you need the same love and attention as always. I've been such a fool. Please forgive me. I can't do this without you, and I never would even want to. Please forgive me."

I could feel my hard heart begin to melt with his words.

"Joe, I want to believe you, but how can I be sure you won't forget again? Can we ever find what we've lost in the past few weeks? I don't know if I can stand our primitive lifestyle much longer. I just never knew it would be this hard."

"We're just going to have to get our priorities in order," he stated matter-of-factly. "Rainy season or not, we're going to have to decide— *I'm* going to have to realize you are more important than the house or anything else and spend more time with you."

"Isn't it weird," I asked, "that we are with each other twenty-four hours a day and still need to spend time together?"

"Well it's true. I've got to set a limit on how much time I work every day, and from now on we're going to take one day a week to enjoy this beautiful place and relax. Deal?"

I sat there on the rock dripping wet. I wanted to believe he would stick to his promise, but I hesitated. "Promise me you'll start noticing what I do accomplish for us so I won't feel like a slave?"

"I already do," Joe insisted.

"Well, I sure don't hear you bragging about the meals I prepare day in and day out, or the fact you have clean clothes and towels every time you reach for them, or that the tent and potty are kept clean, or that. . . ."

Joe interrupted me. "I see what you mean. I'm always so happy when you notice the progress on the house. I just never thought about all the stuff you do every day that I take for granted. I'm sorry. I promise I really will start noticing."

I reached over and hugged his neck. I felt a hundred percent better than I had in weeks.

That afternoon, Joe stopped working at four o'clock sharp. Mercedes went home and Joe made it clear he didn't need to come back that day for anything. *"Hasta mañana!"* he called as Mercedes rowed away.

We ate supper at 4:30, and after cleaning everything up I decided it was time I started enjoying island life. I put on my swimsuit and went down to the lake where Joe was bathing. "Look out below!" I called as I jumped in.

We swam for about half an hour and then went up to watch the sunset. Cory joined us on the step, and we sat fascinated by the brilliant spectacle before us.

"I love you, Joe."

He looked into my eyes and ran his finger down my face and took me into his arms. "I'll always love you and need you, too."

Later that evening, we tried to tune the radio to the VOA. After several adjustments, we heard the welcome sound of English. We listened with enthusiasm to the news and wondered if we could possibly pick up any more English programming.

As we turned the dial back and forth, we tuned in to some kind of drama. Excitedly, we lay in each other's arms and listened to the story of a family who had been broken apart and eventually found happiness together through studying the teachings of Jesus.

"What is this station?" I wondered aloud.

"Shhh, listen," Joe said as the show ended.

There was some static crackling as the announcer identified the radio station, "You are tuned to HCJB, broadcasting from Quito, Ecuador. Welcome to 'Night Sounds.'"

What followed was a half-hour program of soothing music and inspirational comments. As we flipped the radio off, we knew we had found a friend.

"Good night, sweetheart," Joe whispered.

I snuggled against him. "Good night."

TWELVE

Days of Discovery

Our visa and truck permit needed to be renewed and that meant a trip to Managua. I now dreaded those trips to the capital city. Each time the fumes from the traffic, the fast pace, and the unnecessary delays all added up to a headache.

We spent most of the next day waiting to see someone and were then told to come back *mañana*. It was getting late so we decided to see if we could sleep at the Villa Verona, the residence used by University of Tennessee students, instead of having to come back to Managua the next day.

There was an extra twin bed, and we were welcomed. After going to a movie, subtitled in Spanish and eating at a restaurant, I felt as if we'd stepped back into the twentieth century once more.

That night, I went into the huge tiled bathroom to take a shower before bed. I groped around in the dark and suddenly remembered there were electric lights. A look into the huge mirror made me gasp. I looked like some kind of wild woman. I couldn't believe what had happened to me. My skin looked splotchy, my hair was a close match to a broom, and despite the hard work on the island, certain areas of my body definitely needed some exercise.

Gloom settled as I studied myself in the mirror. Then I felt determined. I could change things. First, I'd ask Joe to buy a bigger mirror, and then, I'd set aside a time each day, no matter how busy we were, to exercise and work on improving myself.

The twin bed felt tiny and cramped, and the roar of the air conditioner made it impossible to sleep. I missed our tent and the island sounds, and I wondered if Cory was all right.

"Don't worry about her," Joe said, reading my thoughts. "She survived before us and I'm sure she'll be okay for one night without us."

The next morning, we were eating breakfast with the students when one of them asked me how we kept things cold on the island. As I explained about the block of ice and our cooler, another student jerked his head in our direction and stopped eating.

"Say, I know some folks who might want to sell an old kerosene-powered refrigerator," he said.

"You're kidding?" Joe asked. "How old is it?"

"I don't know, but I can show you where they live. They're missionaries down here, and I'd say it works all right."

I felt elated. The possibility of getting a refrigerator was exciting. I could just imagine ice for tea and fruit drinks. "Oh, Joe, can we go see it?"

"I don't see why not." Then he turned to the student. "As soon as we take care of this paperwork on our passports and the truck, we'll come back and you can show us where these people live, okay?"

"Sure," answered the student.

Everything seemed to go as we had planned for once. We arrived at the office of immigration, and they issued us a one-year permit for the truck and extended our visas.

We left the offices by ten o'clock and headed back to the Villa. The student scrambled into the truck beside me, and the three of us headed up the South Highway—a new road for me.

It was a beautiful drive. We passed several lagoons atop extinct volcanoes and looked down at the sprawling city of Managua.

Soon we turned in a gate beside a high wall. A tanned, gray-haired man came from the cinder block house and greeted us warmly in English, "May I help you?"

Joe and I walked toward him extending our hands. We introduced ourselves. He looked into the truck and waved toward the student.

"Oh, yes," he said, "I remember him from church one Sunday. He came to visit us. By the way, I'm Mel Eberhard."

"Do you have a refrigerator for sale?" I asked.

"Why, yes, it's more than twenty years old, but the last time we used it, it worked fine. There's nothing to tear up on one, so it should keep on operating for a number of years."

He led us around the side of their home, and sitting in the grass beyond the swimming pool was a big, white Servel fridge. I looked inside it
and was surprised that it was in such good shape.

"It will have to be painted, of course," Mel commented, "and I hope
you can find the wicks for it because I only have one extra. But otherwise, it's fine."

"How much do you want for it?" Joe asked hesitantly.

"I believe five hundred cordobas would be a fair price."

Seventy dollars for what we needed as much as anything else on the
island! I was so excited I couldn't speak. All the new ones we had looked
at cost anywhere from five hundred to two thousand dollars.

Joe didn't hesitate. "We'll take it!"

It took the three men and one of Mel's sons to load the bulky appliance into the back of the truck.

"Please tell me everything you can about its operation," I pleaded.

Mel showed us the flat, triangular tank that held the kerosene. Back
in one corner was a wick mechanism much like the one on our kerosene
lantern.

"As the flame heats the alcohol in the closed system of tubing behind
the fridge," he said, "the alcohol circulates and cools the compartment.
At the top of the fridge is a freezing compartment. You can even have
ice!

"Keep the wick trimmed evenly and the flame adjusted to your satisfaction, and you shouldn't have any problems."

We thanked him, paid him the five hundred cordobas, and drove out
of his driveway. We were moving quickly into the twentieth century and
couldn't wait to share our newest convenience with our island friends.
We took the student back to the Villa and hurried on to Granada.

"Can you imagine how much Mercedes and his family will enjoy ice?"
I asked Joe.

"Can you imagine how much we will?" he replied.

We rounded up some reluctant volunteers at the dock to help us load
the fridge into our boat. It was a balancing act to keep it from going overboard as they stepped into the boat, but soon we were slowly plowing
through the water.

Our little friends scurried up on the rocks to dance with Joe as we
drove past their island. They stopped when they noticed the monstrosity

sitting behind us. Then, they began to dance again. Joe let out his finest Tarzan yell, and we waved until they were out of sight.

We finally got the refrigerator working, but the wind kept blowing out the flame. We would smell the kerosene as the wick gave up the battle. Then we remembered the canvas cover we had used on the boat as we drove down.

We tied the canvas in place and waited and hoped. After a couple of hours the refrigerator was actually getting cold. Frost was forming in the freezer compartment.

"Yippee!" I shouted and began to empty the cooler.

"Don't you think we better try the fridge overnight first?" Joe asked, but I was too excited to wait. Sure enough, the flame stayed lit throughout the night, and we had ice the next morning.

In the coming days, the beams were planed, set in place, and bolted to the steel saddles. From the water, our project looked like some kind of wooden Stonehenge mysteriously arranged among the palms.

Joe kept his promise and stopped working each day in time for us to discuss our progress and just talk. We also tuned in each night to our newly discovered radio station.

Then, one morning I turned on the radio and discovered that HCJB had English programming all morning as well as in the evening. We listened with interest to "Morning in the Mountains" and found ourselves searching the Bible in the evenings to find out about the God we were coming to know through our day-to-day dependence on Him and each other.

By the end of March, our routine was comfortable. I wrote,

> To think of the endless race at home in the States is almost beyond our imaginations already. Life here is really simple, even though challenging at times. The sun is the only real "slave driver" around!

Something was beginning to happen to us, and we couldn't quite figure out what it was.

Joe and I were both learning from our island friend. Mercedes was a skilled worker with primitive hand tools. He taught Joe how to use an adz when cutting the beams to fit into the steel joints.

One afternoon Mercedes finally had the opportunity to show me how to fish. He escorted me down to the rocks on the far end of the island where the waves crashed continuously. There in the gravel, he showed me tiny crabs that could be cut in four pieces for fishing bait.

I was jubilant when I caught a ten-inch bass on my first try. He showed me how to filet the fish and we had a delicious supper that night. I finally realized that Mercedes was my friend as well as Joe's.

One morning, Mercedes kept insisting that Joe wear a hat and shirt.

"But why?" Joe kept asking. He'd never worn one before.

Mercedes kept telling him all day that he'd better put on a hat or he'd be sorry, but Joe refused to listen. That night he found out why.

When we got in bed, Joe suddenly had the worst headache he had ever had. He felt sick at his stomach, and we thought maybe he was getting a virus. Neither one of us had been sick since we'd left the States, and I was growing more and more concerned about him.

"I'll be all right," he kept insisting, but neither of us slept very well throughout the night.

The next morning, Joe stepped over to the potty and began to moan in agony.

"What's the matter?"

"There's blood in my urine!"

About that time we heard Mercedes' familiar "Señor Jośe!"

I met him at the top of the steps and explained what was wrong with Joe. His eyes lit up with recognition and he nodded his head. "Sí," he said and with an I-told-you-so expression on his face, he explained that the sun was too hot this time of year to work without a hat as Joe had done the day before.

"The sun is too hot?" I asked. I couldn't imagine it's getting much hotter.

Mercedes pointed to the horizon where the sun was just beginning to peek over the horizon. "Do you see where it is?" he asked me.

I looked and realized that it was rising a noticeable distance to the north of where it had been rising in the past weeks. *How could we be so dumb about nature?* I wondered. *And what a way to learn.*

As we sat down to eat, I looked at Joe's darkened skin and stared down at my own brown arms and legs. "Think our skin can take this abuse?" I asked. "We Americans think we know so much with our fancy college degrees. Mercedes and his family know a lot more about living."

"Yeah," Joe agreed. "There was no way he could convince me that one day in the sun makes that much difference, but, I tell you, he knows about nature, all right."

Over and over again, we were learning valuable lessons from this illiterate native.

In the next few days Joe and I began to plan and work together on the building project.

"What's on the agenda for this week?" I asked one morning.

"Believe it or not," Joe replied, "it's almost time to dig the septic tank. We're going to be able to put the bathroom in as soon as we finish the stone wall on this end of the house."

"Great!" I said enthusiastically. "Then we'll really be civilized again."

The thought of having a real indoor bathroom complete with running water thrilled me. It had been so long since I'd had any privacy, I longed for that more than anything else.

While I was down at the washing rock that afternoon I noticed Mercedes and Joe looking around at the beams standing proudly in place. Then, they bent down and scratched in the dirt.

As I carried the wet clothes out to the far end of the island for drying, I stopped and asked why they were just standing around.

"Well, we've got a little problem," Joe admitted. "I don't know how we're going to hoist the two supporting beams up into the air for the roof. There's no tree close enough to use the block and tackle with."

I thought of tying a rope between the coconut trees, but they had already discussed that possibility and ruled it out. The beams were just too heavy to lift into place without using the block and tackle.

Suddenly, Mercedes got the gleam of an idea in his eye and hopped around. He scampered down to his little dugout tied beneath the spreading ficus tree and said he would be back in a little while.

"*Amigo*, you will be very happy," he called as he rowed away.

"Wonder what he's going to do?" I picked up the laundry again.

"Hard to say," Joe said as he went back to work on the stone wall.

"Why don't you and I start digging the septic tank while he's gone?" I suggested.

"We're really not ready yet—" Joe started, "but—why not? Grab the hoe and shovel, and let's dig."

We broke up the rocky soil behind the house and tossed the dry soil and rocks aside. With every shovelful we were getting closer to my most-wanted room in the house.

We had dug down about two feet when he heard Mercedes calling. We hurried to the steps where we could see him coming. Behind his dugout he was dragging a long, crooked bare-limbed tree.

"What in the world?!" I said as he docked his little boat.

"It's like a crane!" Joe cried in amazement. "It should work perfectly, too!"

"What?" I asked again.

"Look, look," Joe said, grabbing my arm and jumping up and down. "The tree is shaped perfectly to hook the block and tackle at the top of that angled trunk. We can tie off the bottom to the concrete column. It will work!"

Mercedes beamed with pride. He and Joe hacked off all the branches until the tree was just like a telephone pole that was bent at the top in about a sixty-degree angle.

Soon the tall tree was upright and bending over the building site. Amazingly, Joe and Mercedes lifted the massive mahogany beam into the steel joint at the top of the concrete column. Then they tied the rope from the block and tackle around the other end and began hoisting it into place.

"Sandy," Joe screamed, "get that long six-by-six and bring it over here to hold this end in the air until we get the other one hoisted up!"

I grunted and strained trying to drag the long beam to them. Mercedes let go of the rope he and Joe were holding just long enough to help me lift it into place. Then, we braced it again with another rope and beam.

They worked quickly. Moving the tree and the block and tackle to the rear column, they repeated the whole process. Within a few hours, the two supporting beams of our roof were cantilevered in midair ready to be fixed into the steel joint.

"I can't believe how all this goes together!" I yelled at Joe who was atop our huge homemade ladder. "It's just unreal that you could think all this up, have these steel joints made, hand-plane all this lumber, and then fit it all together so perfectly."

"That's what I'm supposed to be able to do," he teased me. "Just don't ask me how to cook a meal! I could never get everything to come out hot at the same time!"

In another couple of hours, the two men got the beams bolted into place. Finally, the real test came. They removed the block and tackle and our tree crane and we held our breath. The beams stood!

We were almost ready for the roof! "Hey, we're going to get the roof on by the rainy season after all, aren't we?" I asked Joe.

He picked me up in his arms and swung me around. "It works; it works!"

"Tomorrow we start putting up the screen for the roof," Joe said as we ate our supper that afternoon. "I hope our plastic in Managua is still good after all this time."

One of the last projects Joe had worked on in school was a park pavilion using the lightweight roofing system we were putting on our house. The leftover barrels of liquid acrylic were somewhere in Managua.

"When will we go to Managua and find out?" I asked. I was a little concerned about the condition of this essential material.

"We'll wait until all the screen is up first," Joe said. "Don't worry. If the plastic is no good, I'm sure we can find it at some company in Managua."

We tuned in to HCJB that evening and listened to another drama. Besides the herons that flew over each afternoon toward their nest on another island, the radio drama was the most entertaining activity of the day. The nightly music and inspiration of "Night Sounds" gave us contact with the rest of the world before we went to sleep.

The next morning we drove over to the Wilsons for the boxes of two-foot screen wire to begin the roof. Mercedes was very curious about this newfangled roof. He couldn't imagine how it was going to work.

It took the next four days to stretch the screen from beam to beam, weaving it in a basket pattern from the two upper beams to the horizontal perimeter beams. In a few places the layers sagged so Mercedes and I sewed them with fishing line. Finally, we had two beautiful hyperbolic parabaloids, double curved surfaces that swept upward like a wave above our island.

We told Mercedes to take the next couple of days off so we could go to Managua and search for the liquid chemical to coat the screen and create a hard fiber glass surface.

We promised two of Mercedes' children a treat from the oven if they would give Cory a fresh fish each day we were away. They readily agreed, so off we went to the "big city."

After going from one warehouse to another and searching several parking areas, we finally found the barrels of plastic that had been there for over a year. Joe cautiously pried one open and lifted the lid. A horrible odor filled our nostrils as we gazed in at the odd-looking liquid.

"There's no way we can stand to smell that, much less use it for the roof," I said in disgust.

"Just hold on. I've got to test it."

Joe filled an empty milk carton with the stinking liquid, and we took it carefully to the office of the Vice Ministry of Urban Planning, the government agency that supervised the University of Tennessee program. One of the men there helped Joe find the additive that made the liquid harden. They experimented for several hours to no avail. The liquid was simply no good after all this time.

I could see Joe was a little disappointed, but he wasn't about to show it. He never gave up so easily.

All I could think about was the unfinished house, our cramped little tent, and the quickly approaching rainy season. "You've got to find something soon," I begged. "What are we going to do?"

"Look," Joe said impatiently. "don't start that whining. I know as well as you do what we have to do. I'm just not going to get upset when I haven't even checked out the alternatives."

I felt hurt by his tone of voice, but I did realize I couldn't do anything about the situation. We rode in silence toward a chemical supplier's business.

Joe explained our problem to the owner, and he shook his head as he thumbed through catalog after catalog. He could see no solution to our problem either. "I'll call Costa Rica in the morning," he assured us. "Perhaps I can order it from there or you two could drive to San José yourselves for what you need."

I felt a little better as we drove toward Villa Verona. All the students gathered around when they heard us enter and bombarded us with questions: "How's the progress on the island coming?" "Are you in the house yet?"

The cook came from the kitchen to ask if we wanted to eat with the students. We were afraid we were wearing out our welcome and insisted we just couldn't. Joe had already told me we would go out to eat, and I was looking forward to that.

We slept in the truck that night, and we were wakened by a storm. I worried about the tent and all our things on the island.

"We don't even know if it rained out there," Joe insisted. "Stop worrying about it."

The next morning we drove back out to the chemical distributor's business. He had called Costa Rica, but without success. The chemical we needed for our roofing liquid simply was not available in Central America.

"Now what?" I asked accusingly as we got back in the truck.

"I'll think of something."

We drove back to the Villa. The students were busy at their drawing boards working on different projects throughout the country.

We explained our problem to an interested young man, and he suddenly had an idea. "Hey, you won't believe this, but we just got word the other day that UT is sending down a new four-wheel drive in the next few days. Maybe the driver could bring you guys the acrylic."

Joe immediately jumped up and ran to the phone.

"What are you doing now?" I asked as he waited for the overseas operator.

"I'm going to see if Dr. Kersavage can get us what we need. I don't care what it takes. I'm going to talk him into it."

I believed him enough to be hopeful. When he finished his conversation, we were both excited. Dr. K was going to do everything possible to be sure we got the material for the roof. It should arrive within the next few weeks.

"A few weeks?" I asked. "But won't that be too late?"

"I don't care when it is, just so long as it gets here," Joe admitted.

We drove back to Granada and decided to go back to our island and work on other parts of the house in the meantime. There was no sense waiting around in Managua. It could take weeks for the new vehicle to arrive.

It felt great to get back to the island. Cory ran up and down every coconut tree, climbed up on top of the tent, and leapt up on the kitchen, then meowed pitifully as we bent to pet her. She was letting us know how much she had missed us.

We resumed digging the septic tank the next morning. As we threw the rocks aside, suddenly I noticed a smooth-looking stone. As I turned it over in my hand, a little round face stared at me. It was the head of a ceramic figurine!

"What's that?" Joe asked as he reached for the artifact.

"I don't know."

We set it aside and continued digging, more slowly and carefully than before. We found several more heads and other pieces of pottery farther down.

We had finally dug a hole that was four by six by seven feet deep. It had taken us two days to do what a backhoe could do in twenty minutes!

We drove into Granada and called Managua from the post office. "Is the plastic here yet?" To our disappointment it wasn't.

We went to the hardware store and picked out the necessary plumbing pieces. We needed a huge tank for storing water and a hand-operated water pump. Finally we had all the necessary parts to have running, pressured water including four long, straight beams to mount a water tower.

As we worked during the next few days, I joyfully anticipated the completion of our water system. Again, our tree crane came in handy as we hoisted the huge tank to the top of the new tower.

Suddenly, Cory came running by. We glanced around to see what she could be running from in such excitement.

We spotted the snake as it slithered into the rocks of the septic hole.

"Get back!" Joe shouted. He was running to get the machete.

I stared at the foot-long brightly ringed snake. It was orange, black, and yellow. "Is that a coral snake?" I gasped.

"I think so!" Joe said, walking toward it cautiously. With one swift movement, he chopped off the snake's head.

"You realize that we could never make it to get help if we were bitten by one of those?" I said.

Joe shrugged his shoulders and shivered. The rest of the day I saw him peering cautiously at every rock, and that night we examined the tent more carefully before we crawled into bed.

In the coming days we killed eight more snakes with Cory's help. She always came running toward us when she spotted one. I hated the fear that had invaded our paradise, but at least we had Cory to warn us of danger.

The three of us were learning to help each other.

Another thing that was happening was that Joe and I were learning all over again to relax and play together as we had done when we were courting in Tennessee.

The following Sunday, I baked a batch of cookies and asked Mercedes if he would trade the use of his smallest dugout for them. Joe and I wanted to row to the base of Mombacho. We had been wanting to explore the hot springs at the bottom of the dormant volcano ever since we arrived in Nicaragua.

He agreed enthusiastically, so about 9:30 we set out across the bay toward the mountain. I had packed us a picnic, and we took turns rowing the little dugout and steering with the extra paddle for a rudder.

After a couple of hours we had finally rowed across the bay and through another group of tiny islands. We eased through the reed-filled water toward the mouth of a small stream. In absolute quiet we rowed slowly through the tall reeds on either side of us.

The stillness surrounded us and left us speechless. In a clearing in the reeds, we looked north toward the dense jungle just a few yards from us. Suddenly, we saw something large moving through the underbrush. We stopped and stared at the creature who climbed a tree and stared back at us.

I'd never seen anything like it. It looked a little like a sloth or an anteater but wasn't either one. We stared until we had memorized the animal's features, and as we reached for our oars, the creature crawled down from the tree and walked slowly away into the dense foliage. I asked Joe what it was, but he didn't know either. We grew silent once more.

I put my hand in the water and quickly withdrew it. The water was hot. The islanders had told us it was hot enough to cook an egg. Now, I knew they were right.

The smell of sulfur filled our nostrils as we rowed on and on up the stream. Then we came to another, larger clearing. Yellow mud lined the banks of the river, and bubbles rose to the surface from the river bottom. We were afloat on a boiling cauldron.

We steered the dugout toward the bank and stepped out into shallow water. My foot burned from the heat of the water and I skittered up toward cooler ground.

"Look at this!" I cried. It was a cleared field marked for playing baseball.

We spread a blanket out at homeplate and enjoyed our picnic lunch. Dense jungle surrounded us. High above on the mountain slopes there were coffee plantations, but in this spot we felt like the only man and woman on the earth.

We watched parrots flitting from one tree to another, and we heard monkey screams and other wild animal sounds in the trees around us. We explored several paths leading into the jungle, but they only led a few dozen feet before stopping abruptly.

I felt so relaxed I couldn't hold my eyes open any longer. "I've just got to take a little nap," I said to Joe as we returned to our picnic spot. He stretched out beside me, and we both went to sleep.

A loud roar awakened us. My heart pounding, I tried frantically to remember where I was. Joe jumped to his feet and peered into the jungle around us. "Must have been a jaguar," he said, "what the islanders call *El Tigre*."

We waited several minutes, but *El Tigre* was not to be seen or heard again. I asked, "Don't you want to try out the water before we head back?"

"You think we can stand it?"

"I don't know, but I sure want to see what it feels like, don't you?"

We walked over to the edge of river and stepped down into the gooey muck along the edge of the bubbling water. My feet and ankles adjusted quickly to the hot water. We stepped out slowly, allowing our legs and thighs to adjust gradually. My skin was covered with a yellow film when I raised my leg to walk.

Finally, we were waist high and we sat back in the yellow mud. "Ooooh! I can't believe how good it feels," I cried with delight. "This is the first hot bath I've had since the States!"

"Gag, I don't see how you can stand it," Joe said. "I'm burning up. I'll take the coolness of the lake any day."

After just about ten minutes, my skin began to itch. As I stood up, the afternoon wind felt cold blowing against my skin. It was the first time I'd felt anywhere near cold in Nicaragua.

We tried to wipe our skin off, but the yellow film remained. We looked like two wild natives loading our gear in the dugout to go home. We glided out from the tall reeds into the lake once more. The sky looked very dark toward the south. What had been a glass-smooth surface in the morning had become a choppy sea.

"How are we ever going to row this little boat across the open lake in these waves?" I asked Joe. I was a little worried about the threatening sky.

"Just keep paddling," he replied.

Raindrops began sprinkling our yellowed skin. I dug deeper and harder into the water with each stroke. The waves were running toward us now. *El chubasco*, as Mercedes called the afternoon rain, was kicking up the water with fury.

Joe was using the steering oar to paddle, too. I sat with my back to the front of the boat, rowing with all my might. "O-E-O Ho-o," Joe began to chant as if he were the slave master on an ancient Viking ship. The rain pelted us harder now. Lightning crashed on Mombachu and steam was rising from the jungles.

I laughed in spite of my fears. Suddenly, I felt confident we could make it no matter what. My body moved in rhythm with his chant, and my arms drove the oar strongly into the rolling waves.

"I love you—you woman, you!" Joe shouted above the wind and thunder.

"I love you, too!"

Each emerald island gave off steaming vapor as the storm passed over. The sinking sun cast long shadows across the water while we rowed past the last few islands toward our own. *El Corazón* glistened in the sunset. Every tree and rock was polished to a high sheen. Steam rose from the massive boulders surrounding our docking area.

"It's good to be home," Joe said as we tied the little dugout to a tree. He put his arms around my waist, and we walked up the steep steps to Cory's welcome home. "Your mama is one doggone good crew," Joe said to her, scratching her head.

"Your daddy's just a good captain," I added.

As we stripped out of our wet clothes and dried off, Joe took me in his arms. "We're quite a team when we work together, aren't we?"

"Aye, aye, Cap'n," I agreed. We both knew something had happened between us that day. We had been one with God's creation and discovered the edge of Paradise.

THIRTEEN

Witch Doctors and Potions

We continued to drive into Granada each day to see if the new vehicle had arrived with our chemical. In the meantime, we worked on our water system and finished up the stonework walls of the house.

Mercedes came late one afternoon and said he needed some time off to visit the huge islands forty miles south of us. Ometepe was a towering volcanic island that towered upward in the middle of Lake Nicaragua. We often saw the rising column of smoke from the far end of our island.

"Wonder why he needs to go down there?" I asked.

"I don't know, but I don't think it's any of our business. He'd have said if he wanted us to know."

We waved to him as he went by in a large dugout the next morning. He and his son Enrique had borrowed our little motor for the trip. We watched them bounce across the gentle waves far out into the open lake. They were just a tiny speck on the horizon when we stopped looking.

That afternoon I was doing the laundry while Joe formed the septic tank top. I looked up and saw Rosa Elena, Mercedes' wife, sitting in a tiny dugout just a few yards from me. Her huge body spilled over the back of the brightly painted boat. She held the sleeping little Mercedes on her lap while she fished with a bamboo pole. She baited the hook and as quickly as she tossed it in the water, she caught a twelve- to fifteen-inch fish. The boat rocked gently with her movements.

I stopped scrubbing and called out to her, "*Hola! Qué tal?*"

Rosa Elena turned the dugout around and waved in response. I motioned for her to come over and called out, "Puedes visitar?" I hoped she understood my bumbling Spanish.

She rowed gently through the water, and Mercedes, Jr., jerked awake and squinted in the sun. Rosa Elena clucked her tongue like a mother hen and smiled. Then she motioned to the pile of laundry and raised her eyebrows. "Yo puedo," she said. I realized she was offering to do the laundry for me and I shook my head. She was staring at the box of detergent on the log nearby. "Qué es?"

I picked up the box and poured the powder out in my hand. It always burned a little, but I had gotten used to it. She touched the powders and shook her head. "No es bueno."

No good? I wondered what she used. Out of her apron pocket she pulled a vanilla-colored piece of soap. "Es mejor!"

I took the soft soap into my hands and looked at it carefully. I had seen the softball-shaped soap in the market, but had never understood how anyone could bathe with such a huge ball of soap. Now I knew what it was for, and I thanked her for telling me.

She stared up the steps to our campsite. I knew she was curious to see the changes we had made since her first visit.

As we walked up the steep steps, Joe looked up from his work and greeted her warmly. Her round tummy shook as she laughed.

She walked around the kitchen admiring the stove, our plywood cupboard, and the refrigerator. I opened the door, and she stuck her hand in to feel the coolness. She laughed again. Then she inspected our wooden table and stools. She liked the stools and said she hoped they could get some soon. They already had a table like ours.

She hesitated at the tent, and I unzipped it and invited her in. She shook her head shyly, but I insisted she step in to see. She ducked down to enter the zippered opening and looked around. "Que lindo!" she said as she pushed on our foam rubber bed. "Que lindo!"

Then, Joe showed her around the building site, and she admired the work Mercedes had done as Joe complimented her husband's ability.

Finally, she came back toward me and walked down the steps to the dock. She turned suddenly and hugged me. I stood there motionless for a second, then hugged her back. "Bienvenidos," she welcomed me warmly. "Bienvenidos."

"Gracias, muchas gracias," I thanked her.

Two days later, Mercedes returned. He came to work bragging about the successful trip. I was glad when he began to tell us why he had gone.

He carefully pulled a handkerchief from his pocket and gently unwrapped it. It was filled with a gray-colored powder. Pieces of white, red, and black particles were ground in with the rest.

"What is that?" Joe asked curiously.

"*Medicina!*" Mercedes announced proudly. Then he went on to explain how he had gone to see the witch doctor at Ometepe for a strong medicine for his eldest daughter, Marta Eugenia.

"*Por qué?*" I asked disbelievingly.

He told us that she had moved away to another island with a boyfriend who didn't want her anymore. But Marta wouldn't leave the island. She was heartbroken and wouldn't eat or sleep. She had moaned and cried for days. Mercedes and Rosa Elena had begged her to come home, but she had refused, kicking and screaming when they tried to pull her into the dugout. Nothing had helped, so Mercedes had gone to the witch doctor as a last resort. He had assured Mercedes that the medicine would heal her and she would easily be persuaded to come home.

"But . . . but . . ." I stammered. I couldn't even think of the correct Spanish words to ask him how he was to administer this miracle powder. Joe found the words for me, and we waited anxiously for Mercedes' reply.

He shielded the powder from the wind and began to describe the different things that had gone into the formula: cat bones, a powerful plant, hair from another animal, special rocks that had been pulverized. . . . On and on Mercedes went, explaining the elaborate preparations. He said the witch doctor charged so much because this was a miracle powder. If he could just slip it in Marta's drink, she would be well.

I sat down on one of the walls of our house. Never in my wildest imaginations had I believed that the stuff I'd read in novels about magic potions could actually be true. My mind reeled. This combination of ingredients could very easily be toxic, if not fatal.

Before I realized what I was doing, I was standing up and speaking in Mercedes' face. My Spanish was flowing as if I'd spoken the language all my life. "Mercedes, there is a God more powerful than the witch doctor. He created this whole world and every plant, animal, and element. He is so powerful that if we just ask Him to do something good for us, He can, and He will because He loves us."

Mercedes listened carefully to every word. He was very interested to hear about this God.

I went on, "The God I'm talking about sent His Son, Jesus, so that we could live in victory over the things in this life that try to get us down. I believe that if we pray and ask Him, He will bring Marta home without the medicine from the witch doctor. Would you like to do that?"

Mercedes listened as a child would listen to a bedtime story. He was eager to talk to this God and followed my eyes as I looked upward and prayed that Marta would come home without the use of this powder.

"En el nombre de Jesus Cristo, amen."

Mercedes smiled and nodded his head. *"Bueno pues,"* he said with confidence as he walked to the edge of the island and opened the handkerchief. The powdery substance blew away with the wind, and I suddenly realized what I'd just done.

Will God really answer our prayer? I wondered. I'd never prayed quite like that before. Joe and I, who had been hearing these nightly dramas on HCJB, had dared to ask God to help a poor native girl on a tiny island in Nicaragua. I still found it hard to believe He had time to care about all these little day-to-day things, but for some unknown reason, I'd uttered my prayer.

I shivered to think of the money and time Mercedes had spent for the witch doctor's potion and dreaded the possibility that our prayer would not be answered.

That night at supper, Joe and I were very quiet. Finally, he spoke. "Sandy, I couldn't believe what you told Mercedes this afternoon. If something doesn't happen soon, he'll never trust us again. I'm not sure even I can believe God will answer prayers about everyday situations."

"I know what you mean, but something just made me want to help him when he started telling us all the stuff in that powder. I was actually afraid of what might happen to Marta if he followed the witch doctor's directions. I've never in my life prayed that way."

"Can you believe what trust he had in the witch doctor?" Joe asked. "And then, when you spoke to him about God, how he just listened and accepted it?"

We listened to the radio again that evening and hoped we had done the right thing. Even though we had thanked God for helping us find my wedding ring and asked for His help in other ways, somehow we always explained the answers away as coincidence.

I lay awake a long time thinking about the past few months and the trials we had come through with each other. *Oh, God,* I prayed, *I hope You are an all-caring God and that You do answer prayers.*

The next morning Joe and I were up long before sunrise. We both kept glancing out toward Mercedes' island, watching for his dugout.

Finally, we saw him coming, and we could hear him singing. "Well, at least he's in a good mood," Joe said as we waited anxiously.

Mercedes hopped out of the dugout and bounded up the steps. His eyes were glowing as he spoke to us. "Amigos, you do know a powerful God," he began in Spanish. "Marta came home last night and is as happy as she ever was!"

"I don't believe it!" I cried in English, and I began to jump up and down.

"Well, praise God!" Joe shouted.

We hugged Mercedes and laughed like children.

FOURTEEN

We Are One

That night as we climbed into bed and turned the radio on, I considered my shallow faith. Over and over Joe and I had experienced direct answers to prayers. We lay there in the darkness listening to the drama unfolding on HCJB.

"Joe," I said quietly, "do you really believe God answered our prayers, or is it all just coincidence?"

"I don't know," he answered, "but I do know that every time we've prayed about things that are important to us or even to Mercedes' family—well, we've gotten a direct answer. It's pretty hard to argue that it could be anything but answers to prayer."

I voiced my deepest fear. "Do you think we've been just halfway Christians?"

I got out of bed and shone the flashlight around the tent looking for some matches to light the oil lamp. I just had to know some things, and I only knew one place to get the answers to our questions.

"What are you doing?" Joe asked sleepily. "We've got a big day tomorrow. The acrylic for the roof may come."

I lit the lamp and the warm glow filled the tent.

"Hey, come on!" Joe blurted out. "I'm worn out tonight. Can't whatever you're doing wait until morning?"

I sat on the closed potty seat and thumbed anxiously through my Bible. I just couldn't wait to find the answers to questions that had been nagging me all day.

"I'll hurry," I promised as I began skimming the New Testament. I skimmed over the "begets" and read on. The words of Jesus were printed in red and I quickly read a few chapters.

Suddenly my eyes were drawn to a particular group of verses, Matthew 7:7–12:

> Ask, and it shall be given you; seek, and ye shall find; knock, and it shall be opened unto you:
> For every one that asketh receiveth; and he that seeketh findeth; and to him that knocketh it shall be opened.
> Or what man is there of you, whom if his son ask bread, will he give him a stone?
> Or if he ask a fish, will he give him a serpent?
> If ye then, being evil, know how to give good gifts unto your children, how much more shall your Father which is in heaven give good things to them that ask him?
> Therefore all things whatsoever ye would that men should do to you, do ye even so to them; for this is the law and the prophets.

I read it over again.

"You've just got to let me read you something," I said cautiously to Joe. He lay with his arm shielding his eyes from the lamplight.

"Okay," he agreed impatiently.

"Isn't it simple?" I asked him after reading. "We just asked, and, sure enough, the Lord gave! And isn't that easy to understand about how He wants to give us good things?"

"It sounds simple," Joe admitted, "but surely there must be more to it than that. We'll have to study it and try what the verse says. We'll find the answers if we seek. Right now, I'm too tired to think, and I'm hoping the acrylic comes soon so we aren't stuck in this tent through the rainy season."

I closed the book and blew out the lamp.

"Well, God," I prayed quietly, "Joe is tired, and we're both getting anxious to get out of this tent. Please help the new vehicle with the acrylic to get here soon. I pray in Jesus' name, amen."

I felt like a child on Christmas Eve as I struggled to go to sleep. Could it be possible that the God who created all things really cared about all our little problems? I was anxious to discover the answer.

The next morning we got ready to go into town. Mercedes arrived at his usual time and began to collect flat-sided rock for the perimeter walls of the house.

When we called Managua from the post office, the vehicle still had not arrived.

We got back to the island by midmorning. I was terribly discouraged. Joe was quiet and I knew he was getting very impatient.

After lunch we were doing rockwork on the house walls when we noticed one of the tour launches heading our way.

"Wonder who in the world that could be?" I asked as I squinted to see.

The launch was full of people. Mercedes and Joe cleaned the cement off their hands as the group came closer and closer.

I rushed out to take down the laundry. As I took the last sheet from the line and turned back toward the tent, one of the tallest men I'd ever seen began climbing the steps to the upper level of the island.

Mercedes stopped what he was doing and stared as if he were seeing a mythical giant. Sure enough, when the young man was only halfway up the steps he was as tall as I am.

Another came behind him. And another. Accompanying the group was Mr. Eberhard, the missionary who had sold us our refrigerator.

Joe isn't short, but even at six feet tall, he was a shrimp compared to these guys. I just couldn't imagine who they were.

With a rather dazed smile on his face, Joe greeted each one warmly. "Welcome to *El Corazón*."

Mel stepped forward from the end of the line and shook Joe's hand. He, too, was dwarfed beside the young men. "This is the exhibition basketball team made up of all-stars from all over the world. They're on tour and giving a demonstration game in Managua."

Suddenly it was clear. I tried to explain to Mercedes about basketball, but he wasn't familiar with the game. He continued to stare at the men with his mouth open and muttering, *"Gigantes!"*

They were all filled with questions and we tried to tell them the why's and how's of life on a Nicaraguan island. After about an hour's visit they ambled back down our stone steps to the waiting launch.

As we waved good-by, Joe told Mel to feel free to surprise us any time. Once they were out of sight we tried to get back to work, but Mercedes couldn't stop talking and laughing about seeing a whole family of giants. From then on, Joe and I enjoyed a new awe in Mercedes' eyes because we knew the "giants."

Near the end of March, we had tremendous wind off the lake. The driving dust turned the side of our bright blue and yellow tent a dirty brown. If I didn't wet down the kitchen area every few hours, a thin layer of dust would settle on the table, the food supplies, and every flat surface.

One afternoon, Mr. Wilson and Mario surprised us with a visit and a mango pie. Mario sauntered around the island obviously curious about everything we were doing.

"Thanks so much for the pie!" I exclaimed. "I've never even tasted a mango."

Mr. Wilson jerked his head around.

"You're kidding, aren't you?" he asked in disbelief. "We make a lot of income each year on our mangoes. When they're green they're like apples, and when they're ripe they're better than a peach."

He walked over to where Joe and Mercedes were applying a dark stain to the mahogany beams and peered up at the two towering beams outlined against the sun. "What in the world are you going to do here?" he asked hatefully.

Joe tried to explain the roofing system to him, but Mr. Wilson just shook his head.

"It'll never work, young fellow," he said. "You two are wasting your time. You better get you some tin and put a real roof on this thing!"

Mario mimicked him and stood shaking his head and clucking his tongue as though to reinforce Mr. Wilson's view of our stupidity. When Mr. Wilson removed his cap and scratched his head, so did Mario.

Joe moved toward the tent. "Where's the drawing of the house?" he asked as he rummaged around under the bed. He was pulling boxes from underneath our plywood bed and strewing things all over the floor of the tent that I had just finished sweeping.

"Joe, can't you be careful?" I asked anxiously.

He sat down on the floor and squinted at me through the zippered opening. Perspiration streamed down his face.

"I've got to have that picture to show him," he said through gritted teeth. "If he and Mario keep acting like they know it all, I'm going to be really angry."

Suddenly I remembered where I had stored the drawing. I went into the tent and reached under the foam rubber pad on the bed.

"Here it is," I said coolly, looking at the mess on the floor and feeling angry at myself for not remembering sooner.

Joe ducked through the tent opening and proudly displayed the drawing of the finished house to Mr. Wilson and Mario. Mario watched Mr. Wilson's face to see what he would do next. Mr. Wilson's eyes grew round as he stared at the drawing. Abruptly, he handed the drawing to Joe and announced he had to go home.

As he and Mario walked by the kitchen I said, "Be sure to tell Bea that I appreciate the pie!"

They both stomped down the steps and jumped into their boat. They sped away without so much as a good-by wave.

"What happened to him?" I asked.

"I guess it got to him to see a young whipper-snapper like me who knows what he's doing!" Joe said haughtily. "It made him mad to see how well we're doing."

"Well, he did act strange," I admitted. Then I remembered the mess in the tent.

"You're gonna pick up all that stuff, aren't you?" I asked.

"Oh, come on, Sandy," Joe answered. "You don't have anything else to do right now. I've got to get back to staining. Can't you pick it up? You know how all of it goes."

I glared at him as he turned and walked back over to Mercedes. "You make me so mad when you say something like that!"

Mercedes looked up with a twinkle in his eyes. He watched both of us. I was embarrassed and slung the zippered flap on the tent as I went in to begin picking up the mess.

I stared at the scattered books on the floor. "When is he going to learn that I'm not his maid?" I muttered under my breath as I stuffed the books back under the bed.

I sat there on the blue-plastic floor and stared at some ants winding their way toward the kitchen. Looking at their tiny bodies made me realize the tedious effort of trying so hard to adjust to this lifestyle. I felt so alone and homesick. *How can I say that?* I asked myself. *I'm on a beautiful island with the man I love! I have no debts to pay, no health problems, no hunger. Why in the world am I not happy?*

I glanced at the open Bible lying on the trunk where I had left it the night before. *Could that ancient book really hold answers to my deepest longings?* For nights we had listened to dramas, music, and inspiration on radio station HCJB. I always appreciated other people's stories of finding God but usually forgot them with the rising sun and the next day's endless chores.

If I did begin to study and dig for answers, would Joe have the desire to learn? He always seemed so happy anyway. Maybe I had different needs that I'd just have to live with. I didn't want to discover something that I couldn't share with Joe.

My mind reeled with thoughts I'd never even tried to express to Joe. I thought back to the year before when I had been so excited about the island plans. I had dreamed of having a beautiful tan, lazy days in Joe's arms, and no pressures from anyone. Oh, sure, I had known we would have to work hard to make the dream become reality, but always in the back of my mind had been that picture of two beautiful people, madly in love with each other with nothing coming between them.

"Here I sit in an eight- by ten-foot tent cleaning up a mess made by somebody who hardly carries on a decent conversation with me," I said under my breath. "What kind of marriage is this?"

Tears escaped from my eyes as I lay on the tent floor and stared at the open Bible.

"Sandy!"

Joe's voice shattered my sleep. I jerked my head upward and tried to focus. My body was stiff from lying on the hard-packed earth beneath me.

"Are you okay?" Joe asked as he peered in the opening.

"Yeah," I said drowsily, "I must have gone to sleep."

"I'll say," Joe said as he unzipped the tent and stepped in. "It's nearly four o'clock and I'm getting hungry. What are we going to have for supper?"

I dropped my head back down on my arm and stared at nothing in particular. Suddenly all the thoughts in my mind before I had fallen asleep came flooding back like a tidal wave. I couldn't speak.

"Come on," Joe urged me, "get a move on. You don't want to have to cook in the dark, do you?"

I wanted to scream but felt it was useless. What could I say that I hadn't already told him a few weeks ago. Regardless of the few times he had tried to appreciate what I was doing, Joe really hadn't changed. In his mind, each of us had a certain role and I was failing at mine.

He went down to the water for his afternoon ritual. I could hear him splashing around and letting out his Tarzan yell.

I dragged myself to the kitchen and stared into the refrigerator. I couldn't think of anything to fix and longed for a fast-food restaurant. A few weeks ago I had been happy to have the propane stove and then the refrigerator had given me joy. But where was my happiness now?

I threw something together and watched Joe wolf it down. He jabbered on and on about how beautiful the stained beams were. "Isn't it beautiful?" he asked at one point but didn't wait for a reply.

Finally we were in bed, trying to tune in our nightly radio program. Try as we might, we could not get the station. Oddly, I was relieved. I didn't really want to hear how God had blessed others when I was beginning to doubt so many things.

"What's wrong, honey?" Joe asked, turning toward me.

I shrugged my shoulders and didn't dare look at him. I didn't know how to begin to explain my dilemma and just longed to escape again into sleep.

"Come on, Sandy," Joe pleaded. "Tell me what's bugging you. Did I do something to make you mad, or are you just homesick?"

"I don't know," I answered.

We lay there in silence for a long time, the waves crashing on the rocks and the wind whistling through the palm trees. Cory wormed her way into the tent through an opening in the zipper. She gently hopped onto the bed and curled up at our feet. Looking at her made me feel even more discontented.

I turned toward the screened window above my side of the bed. I looked out into the moonlit night. *Oh, God,* I prayed silently, *if you're really there please help me find the joy I thought I'd have with Joe.*

"Good night," Joe whispered as he kissed me.

"G'night," I mumbled.

The next morning we prepared to leave for town. "Maybe today," Joe said, hoping the acrylic had arrived. I sliced each of us a piece of the mango pie Mr. Wilson had brought the day before. It was delicious, and I added mangoes to my shopping list.

Joe gave Mercedes his instructions before we left. As I stepped into the boat, Joe hopped in and cranked the motor. I fell into my seat and stared ahead. My heart was still full of discontent. On the way in we passed Rosa Elena sitting in the tiny dugout, catching one fish after another. Two of the children were with her.

"How does she do it?" I asked Joe as we waved and swerved around them.

"She knows what bait to use," he answered.

I just rolled my eyes and looked away. *He thinks I'm referring to her fishing! Doesn't he even see?*

"What's the matter with you?" Joe said loudly above the roar of the motor. "I'm getting pretty aggravated. I try to find out what's bugging you, and you just clam up. Now, you're mad about something else. I can't read your mind, you know."

I didn't want to yell over the sound of the motor, so I just sat there staring at the water. "Look out!" I screamed as we narrowly missed a protruding boulder.

Joe swerved the boat sharply. "You'd better watch where you're going!" I yelled. "If anything happens to this motor, what would we do then?"

He didn't answer. His face had a hard look of determination. We passed the island with the dancing children scampering on the rocks, but Joe didn't even notice.

Finally we reached the dock and Joe went immediately to the post office to call about the acrylic. I could see his face as he talked into the receiver. From his disappointed look I knew the answer was no.

He didn't speak as he climbed back into the truck.

"What are we going to do if that stuff doesn't come?" I asked sullenly.

"Look," Joe capitulated, "I can't keep working like I have been to get this house built if you're not going to support me in it." He looked at me for a moment and went on. "For days something has been bugging you, and I don't know what it is, but I want it to stop. Whatever you have on your mind, spit it out! I don't think I can be happy for both of us much longer."

My face reddened. Tears stung my eyes. I crossed my arms and leaned against the door on my side of the truck. What could I tell him? I didn't know myself.

"Sandy," Joe said reaching for my arm, "please tell me what's wrong."

"I don't know," I replied. "I just don't know."

He started the truck and drove around the central park on the way to the market. I couldn't bear to look at him. *What is happening to us?* my thoughts cried out. *What happened to that dream of paradise we tasted just a few weeks ago?*

Later, when we returned to the island, I was determined to find some answers. I went into the tent and sat down on the potty. *Pitiful!* I thought. *The only comfortable place to sit on this whole island is a porta-potty!*

I looked around the tiny area we had called home for four months. A year ago Joe had estimated we'd be living in our island house within four months. He'd been wrong about that, too.

Beside me lay my Bible where I'd left it open nights before. A layer of dust coated the pages. I blew them off and stared at the words printed in red. There was the passage I'd read about asking and seeking.

O, God, I prayed quietly, *help me find some answers. I'm asking You and trusting that You're really there to help me in my search. In Jesus' name, amen.*

I stared at the words and began to read at verse 24 where I'd stopped. "Therefore whosoever heareth these sayings of mine, and doeth them, I will liken him unto a wise man, which built his house upon a rock. . . ."

I was astonished at the simplicity of Jesus' statement. If I could read His sayings and begin to do them, He was promising that no matter what—our house would stand! I read on with eagerness. I wanted to read all of His sayings. Never had the Bible seemed so clear. The more I read, the more I felt as if we were living in New Testament days.

On and on I read. Those people must have been bewildered by Jesus and the miracles happening before their very eyes. Certainly I'd heard these stories in Sunday school as a child, but now they were more than stories. These were real people with real problems. Jesus forgave their sins, healed their broken bodies, even raised some from the dead, and all the time He taught them about the kingdom of heaven.

I glanced up and noticed Joe's watch hanging from the support poles. Three o'clock! Time to prepare our afternoon meal. Regretfully I put the Bible down and left the tent.

"You take a nap?" Joe called from across the island.

"No," I answered, stretching and yawning, "I was just reading." I wondered if Joe would feel the same way I did when he read these accounts from the Bible. I wanted to share them with him, but lately it had been too hard to talk with him about important things.

Cory scampered toward me and rubbed my leg with her arched back. "Guess you're getting hungry, too?"

As I stooped to pet her, she scampered up the coconut tree across the top of the tent and onto the top of the pantry box. "You little show-off!" I cried, chasing her off. She hopped up on the table and lay down to watch curiously as I prepared the meal.

After Mercedes left we ate quietly. For the first time in days, Joe was silent. No talk about the house or construction or anything.

"Joe," I finally said, "I was reading something important today." I waited for him to comment, but he just kept on eating. "You've just got to read it, too. I don't know what I'll do if we can't discuss it. I've got to know if what I'm reading is really true or if I'm just the gullible type."

"What are you talking about?" Joe asked. "I don't know from one day to the next what your mood is going to be. One day you're happy and seem to love being here, and the next you're crying and homesick. I'm really confused. Can't you just be happy with each day?"

I could feel the tears welling in my eyes. I fought to hold them back. "I don't know, either," I answered. "I'm trying so hard to understand why I'm like this." I couldn't hold back the tears any longer. I was crying and didn't know exactly why.

"Now what?" Joe asked in disbelief. "You're the one who started this conversation. What's got you upset this time?"

I stood up and ran from the table to the end of the island where the wind dried the tears on my cheeks as quickly as they fell. I hugged myself and stared out across the water. My head was beginning to throb. "Why can't I be consistent?" I asked myself. "Why do my moods change so much? I've never been like this before."

It was dark as I made my way toward the tent, the oil lamp sending out a welcome glow from the screened windows. Joe was already in bed, reading. I washed my face, arms, and legs and brushed my teeth. When I unzipped the tent, Joe glanced up. "You feeling better?" he asked.

"I don't know," was all I could offer. I dressed for bed and crawled across Joe to my side.

"Did you notice what I'm reading?" Joe asked as he blew out the lamp.

"No, I didn't."

"I don't want you to know something I don't, so I've been reading the book of Matthew, too. It really is amazing how the life surrounding us is like New Testament times, isn't it?"

I couldn't believe it! So he wanted to know, too! I felt so happy inside—he had observed the same thing. "Oh, Joe, I love you!"

"Hey, that's what I want to hear!"

The next morning I felt terrible. My head ached and I felt too tired to move.

"Sandy," Joe called, "we need to go to Granada again and call about the acrylic. I sure hope it's in." He peeked into the tent and stared at me. "What's the matter?"

"I'm not feeling so good," I answered weakly. Then I realized what it was. "Oh, gosh, that's all I need," I moaned.

Joe looked puzzled for a minute, then nodded his head. "I thought there must be something physically wrong these last few days. At least you won't have to worry about whether or not you're pregnant anymore."

I turned over and cried with relief. As much as I wanted children, I certainly didn't want them on this island. I was glad I wasn't pregnant in one way but disappointed in another. I'd never had regular menstrual cycles and now the combined heat and humidity made this period especially uncomfortable.

I felt ugly and bloated for several days, but Joe seemed especially relieved.

"How can you be so sure that's what had me so upset?" I asked.

"It had to be!" he said. "You're just not usually that pessimistic. From now on when you start feeling especially low and tired, I'm going to realize it might not be my fault. It could just be your hormones."

I hoped he was right.

For several days we worked as hard as ever to complete the perimeter walls and install the water and the septic system.

Still no word about the acrylic. But we had one thing to celebrate in April. Joe's birthday! We made a trip to Managua and headed out to the beach. It was my first trip to the Pacific coast in Nicaragua, and the black sand beach was a real surprise.

I felt terrible because I didn't have an elaborate gift for Joe. In the two years I'd known him, my family and I had made a big deal at birthday time. This year I had neither time nor money to shop for anything special.

"Don't worry about it!" he insisted. "I'm just glad to get a day off in the middle of the week! Besides, the sand they delivered to the island yesterday was the best present I could get."

It felt great to get back to the island. As much as we always enjoyed the ocean, the fresh water around the island was much more refreshing.

The next morning Joe had to tell Mercedes we wouldn't be needing him to work full-time any more. Our money was dwindling rapidly, and until the roof material arrived, there just wasn't enough to keep two men busy.

Mercedes graciously accepted the news and went home. I sadly realized he'd probably never had such a steady job with good pay before.

Joe and I worked together all day. We shoveled, raked, and leveled the rocky soil to make the foundation of the interior floor ready for tile. Of course, tiling would have to wait until the roof was finished, but the preparation could be done.

In the afternoon, we stopped working at four o'clock and jumped in the water. I was gradually overcoming my fear of sharks.

"We need to make a float of some kind so we can lie around here in the water," Joe decided one afternoon.

"Why don't we just buy an air mattress?" I asked.

"Yeah!" Joe agreed. "Next time we're in town let's get one."

Next time turned out to be the next morning. In Granada we stopped first at the post office for our mail and the phone call to Managua. Still no acrylic, but at least we had mail. A tape from Dad and a letter from Joe's mom.

We went to the hardware store since it always had everything. We entered the cool, dark *ferreteria* and looked around at the myriad of equipment, tools, and appliances. I searched the walls and shelves but couldn't see any air mattresses displayed.

Joe walked to the counter. Five young fellows crowded to serve him. All of them chorused, *"Que quieres?"*

As Joe tried to describe the item, they all began laughing. They had obviously never heard of one. "I guess we'll just have to make one!" he said to me.

We walked back out to the truck quietly as Joe's imagination began to design something that would float. I glanced up and down the crowded street. People were rushing everywhere. It seemed to me that at least one of every three women was pregnant or carrying a tiny baby.

Most people wore plastic shoes or none at all. Many of the men wore slick, brightly printed shirts or neat, pleated short-sleeved shirts in pastel colors. People smiled and talked cordially. It seemed that no one was a stranger.

"I've got it!" Joe interrupted my thoughts. He was busy sketching something on the back of an envelope. I looked at his plans.

"What in the world? . . ."

"Well, I know it will work," he assured me. "If we buy two pieces of plywood and sandwich a piece of styrofoam in between, then wrap them in canvas and paint it with a waterproof paint, we'll have ourselves a float!"

Back we went to the *ferreteria* to buy our needed supplies. The young fellows inside jumped to our assistance, and within minutes we were hauling our new toy to the back of the truck.

That afternoon, as excited as two children, we began to build our float, and by the next morning we were almost done. I was pushing a long needle through the canvas to sew the sandwiched layers together.

"It sure is nice to work on something that will actually be completed in a couple of days rather than months, isn't it?"

"You know," Joe agreed, "you're absolutely right."

We painted it that afternoon and were anxious for the next day. Sure enough, when we carried it down to the water and tossed it in, the contraption floated.

No sooner had we jumped on than Cory was on the rocks meowing loudly. We paddled our float toward her and called for her, but she balked at jumping and ran up to the tent.

There was one problem. The current kept carrying us away from the island. We couldn't relax because we had to keep paddling ourselves back to the island.

"Hey," I shouted, "why don't we tie a rope from the tree to the raft so we won't drift?"

As we paddled to the huge ficus tree we noticed the low level of the water on the boulder we used to dock the boat.

"Had you seen how much lower the water is getting?" I asked.

"Gosh, no," Joe answered. "We probably ought to go on and build a permanent docking area, especially since the roof material hasn't arrived yet. And that would give Mercedes some extra work to finish paying for that dugout he's having built."

We floated around on our homemade platform and studied the rocks and water movement. We agreed on the ideal location for our dock and dived around to check for any boulders that would interfere with the boat or swimming.

For the next few days, Mercedes again reported to work and stacked rock all day long. Once he and Joe had exhausted the supply of rock that could easily be carried from the island, they began to dive for more. The dock was taking shape at an amazing speed. A long ramp extended out from the leeward end of the island and gently sloped to allow for water fluctuation.

In the meantime, we spent our evenings reading and studying and listening to HCJB when we could find it.

We had finished the gospels of Matthew and Mark and were busy comparing Luke's version with theirs. We were constantly amazed at the simplicity of their writings. One night, having just begun John's gospel, we came to the third chapter where Nicodemus was talking with Jesus in the night.

The words "born again" seemed to leap from the page. I had always associated those words with certain denominations. In my church we had been taught to believe, confess, be baptized, and take communion— and that was all there was to knowing God and obeying Him.

Now, I was learning much more than I'd ever known. Living in the open, surrounded by water, beautiful flowers, and brilliantly colored birds, Joe and I both were realizing that God had much more in His plans for human beings than just Sunday morning religion. He called believers to a lifestyle, an intimate walk with a heavenly Father that we'd never before experienced. Time and again we had read the words, *Ask and it shall be done,* and Joe and I both wanted that kingdom of God within us.

"Sandy," Joe said taking my hand one warm night toward the end of April, "I'm not exactly sure what we're getting into, but I know I believe this Book when it says, 'He who gains the whole world and loses his soul has gained nothing.' I don't want to build anything on this island, in our marriage, or elsewhere if it means losing out on the tremendous blessings we've read about. If you're ready, I am! Let's make a commitment right now to make Jesus Christ the Lord of our lives."

My eyes filled with tears as I grasped Joe's hand. At that moment we heard the familiar sound of the foghorn introducing "Night Sounds" from HCJB. In the solace of that sound we stared up into the star-filled, velvet night.

"Oh, God, our Father," Joe said shyly, "Your word has become so real to Sandy and me. You know better than we do what You've already done for us and all that lies ahead in the future. I just pray that You will accept my apology for being impatient with Sandy at times, for being so demanding, for losing my patience with Mr. Wilson—oh, there're so many things I need forgiveness for, but most of all, for not making Your Son, Jesus Christ the boss over every area of my life.

"Your word says that I just have to confess with my mouth and commit my way unto You and You will do what You've said. So, I just want everything You've got for me on this earth."

I could feel Joe's heart beating as he spoke. He squeezed my hand to indicate he had said all he wanted to say. My throat had a lump in it as I opened my mouth to speak.

"Oh, God," I began, "I, too, want Your Son Jesus Christ to be my Lord. Years ago I said I believed in Him, but now I know how much I need You and how much I can't handle my life on my own. You know how I've cried out to You so often in these past few months. I've been so lonely, Lord, even though I ought to be the happiest woman in the world.

"Please, show me the kingdom You spoke of in the New Testament. I want all You have to give."

It seemed so simple. We lay there in silence for a long time. There were no fireworks, no flash of lightning, no signs from the heavens—just the gentle lapping of the waves on the rocky shore of our tiny island. The wind rustled the palm branches above, the same as before. Cory still lay curled at the foot of our bed.

But something had changed within us. The peace was palpable. The love that flowed between Joe and me was perfect contentment. We could not even speak.

FIFTEEN

One with God's Universe

The next morning I half expected angels to be sitting at the table. Instead the empty water jug was waiting, and the same old chores still had to be done. I grabbed the kettle and turned to go down to the water.

As I turned I felt an uneasy feeling smack dab in the middle of my body. It was the same kind of feeling I remembered having before going onstage as a child. I slowed down, but the feeling was still there.

I knelt down to fill the kettle, and the word *rejoice* came to me. I was puzzled. Rejoice? What could it mean?

I trudged back up the steps to the kitchen and looked down at the crude wooden table and stools, the plywood pantry we called our kitchen, the stove sitting on the hard-packed earth, and the fridge. *Rejoice?* I suppose I could. The muscles in my brow relaxed. I hadn't even realized they were tensed. My neck and shoulders loosened in the next moment. *Am I always that tense?* I asked myself.

Mercedes and Joe were down in the water diving for rocks. I looked at the dock they were working so hard to build. *Certainly I can rejoice about that!* I beamed. *No more contortionist's movements to unload the boat. A sheltered area for swimming!*

I stared down the lake toward Mercedes' island. There was Rosa Elena in her usual spot, floating around in the dugout with at least two of the children, fishing in order to live. Rejoice! We had more in savings than they might ever see! Suddenly, almost miraculously, my attitude was changing.

After breakfast, I sat on a rock and stared in amazement at the long list in the concordance in my Bible under the word *rejoice.*

About noon Joe stomped up the steps and grinned at me. He was dripping wet. His faded orange gym shorts drooped around his hips. "You wanna go into town and check on the acrylic?" he asked.

"It doesn't matter," I answered. "I can wait until in the morning if you want to. Then I can go to market, too."

"You seem so much more relaxed today, Sandy," Joe commented as he walked over to see what I was reading. "Even your face looks different."

I smiled happily at him. For the first time since we'd been in Nicaragua, I actually felt at home. I stared at the stately beams standing upright in the diamond shape of our house.

Jumping up, I grabbed my palm frond broom and hurried over to the chunks of rock and soil still needing to be leveled before we could possibly have a floor. I began to clear away the larger masses and sweep the area smooth.

"I'm glad someone's got some energy around here!" Joe shouted as he emerged from the tent. "I can hardly lift my arms after moving all that rock."

"You deserve a rest," I said. "I just wish I could offer you a comfortable seat besides the potty!"

"Why don't we buy a hammock in Masaya tomorrow morning?" Joe asked as he walked toward the windy side of the island. He stared upward at two towering palms. "These two trees are perfectly spaced for a hammock. I don't know why we haven't done it before."

In the next few days, the island became more and more the place we'd always dreamed it could be. Finally one morning Joe made the habitual call to Managua, and I could see from his expression that the news was good. The young man who was delivering the vehicle had called from Guatemala that morning and was due to arrive the next morning.

After giving Mercedes and a couple of the children instructions on looking after Cory and *El Corazón*, we drove to Managua early the next day. I scooted over close to Joe, something I hadn't done since we'd driven down from the U.S.

"Hey, baby!" he wheedled as he put his arm around me and hugged me, "where you been?"

"Over yonder," I said motioning to the passenger side.

"Well," Joe chortled, "like the ole feller in the mountains said to his hundred-year-old wife, 'Jez remember I ain't never moved!'"

There was the usual hustle of traffic in Managua. The diesel fumes always made me nauseous, and I could feel the tension returning to my face, neck, and shoulders.

Finally, we pulled up to the villa, but there was no sign of a new vehicle. The students assured us it should arrive at any minute, but I was not upset. I had learned to be prepared for a night away from home whenever we left the island. Sure enough, we ended up sleeping in the truck.

Late the next afternoon, two weary students pulled up to Villa Verona. We barely spoke before we hurried to the vehicle and peered in. "There it is!" we chorused, jumping around in each other's arms.

But as we stared at the huge drum of gooey liquid, I wondered how in the world we'd get the stuff out to the island. The lid had loosened in one place and some of the acrylic was oozing down the side of the brown barrel and making a puddle on the floor. At least it didn't smell bad.

"Boy, we had a time explaining that stuff at the borders," one of the students said wearily. "I'm sure glad we made it. I thought the guards at the Guatemalan border were going to have a fit before they let us through."

We couldn't thank them enough. It took four of the students to help Joe get the heavy barrel loaded in the back of our camper.

As we bumped along the roads out of Managua the sky looked threatening toward the south. Huge dust clouds were swirling above the flat, open fields. Thick brown dust covered every yard and house. Nicaragua needed rain badly, but I hoped we would have a roof before the rains came.

Just before we arrived in Granada, the rain started. Huge drops pelted our windshield as the dark black clouds passed overhead. In a few minutes the trees turned bright green and lifted their branches upward. The road began to steam around us.

Instead of seeking shelter, the people of Granada were out in full force. Children were dancing in the rain. The old women who sold food at the central park were laying out metal bowls to catch the falling water. Everyone was smiling.

Joe squeezed my hand and said, "Don't worry. If the tent leaks, everything will have time to dry out before nightfall."

I tried not to think about it. There was nothing I could do about it anyway.

"We'll wait until tomorrow morning and hire a launch to bring out the acrylic," Joe commented as we pulled into Puerto Asese.

The few islands that surrounded the dock were shimmering with raindrops. Never had I seen them look so beautiful. Every rock gleamed as if it had been polished. Towering Mombacho was hidden by cloudy vapors. The water had turned muddy brown along the shoreline, but seemed clearer than ever out in the bay.

"Look," I shouted. "Look how beautiful the islands are now!"

We jumped into the boat and sped away. The "dancing" children scurried about when they heard our motor pass their island. Joe danced a jig for them, and they waved joyfully. Their little brown bodies were shining clean, and their black hair was slick and dripping.

As we rounded the peninsula, our little jewel shone in the water. Cory came scampering down to the dock and stretched as she waited for us to dock the boat.

I jumped out, picked her up, and ran up the slick stone steps to the tent. The outside was streaked with mud where the rain had moistened the dirt. A little puddle gathered at the zippered opening. I stepped inside and began to feel the bed first. Only one corner seemed to be wet. "How is everything?" Joe called.

"Seems to be okay," I said as I stepped from the tent and walked over to inspect the kitchen hut. Everything was wet, but nothing was ruined. The pilot light was out on the stove but that didn't matter. I stooped to check the refrigerator and was surprised to see that its wick was still lit.

It was quiet. I could hear the rain dripping from the leaves of the plum tree above me, and the lake was strangely still.

I was thankful that nothing had been damaged. It was May 22, and we had survived our first tropical storm without the house. I hoped we wouldn't have too many more before we would be safe and snug under a real roof.

The next several days were hectic. We climbed up and stapled the screen wire across the beams to make a solid surface. Then, while Joe hired a launch to haul the acrylic and two smaller containers of additives to the island, Mercedes and I sewed up more places that had begun to sag since the storm. Little palm buds had been blown everywhere and it was a job trying to pick them out of the screen. Joe, who wanted the roof to be perfect, was pleased with the work.

Finally, on May 27—our five-month anniversary—we were ready to begin coating the screen with the sticky acrylic that would harden into a roof surface.

Joe looked at the sky. There was no way to know whether or not it would rain by looking. The storms came so quickly there were only minutes to get prepared.

"Weren't we reading about the Lord's promise to do what two people agree on, or something like that?" he asked me.

"Yes," I answered, "what do you have in mind?"

"This roof is pretty important," Joe answered, "and I just want everything to go well. If we have any rain while we're spreading the coating, we'll have a mess. Will you agree with me to ask the Lord to hold off the rain for just a few days until the roof is coated?"

I was a little leery, but decided it certainly wouldn't hurt. "I guess if the Bible says something, it must be true. And I don't remember reading that you can't ask for good weather! That's the least we can do. Yes! I believe our heavenly Father wants to give His children good things and that He'll help us with this."

"Then it's settled," Joe said matter-of-factly. "On with the show!"

Mercedes helped me mix the acrylic, carefully measuring the liquids into a huge bucket. Joe was ready with several squeegees to spread the liquid over the screen wire.

"*Ahora, soy un químico!*" Mercedes bragged, flashing his grin.

"Yeah," I joked with him, "you look like a chemist!" He wore his patched polyester pants and his faded baseball cap. What would Joe's stepfather, a chemist at Tennessee Eastman, think of this kind of chemist?!

We worked all day, taking only a few minutes to eat sandwiches. The sun was hot and there was hardly any wind. Thankfully there was no sign of rain from the south.

By the end of the day, one whole side of the roof was coated. Joe had flakes of dried acrylic all over his hands and arms. Exhausted, we fell into the lake to wash off and went to bed.

For three days we mixed, moved scaffolding, and squeegeed the coating. There was no rain. Our prayer had been answered and we rejoiced.

Natives we'd never seen before appeared in their dugouts around our island each day. They fished and stared at the work on our crazy-looking house. Many of them would call to Mercedes and ask him what kind of church we were building.

Even the launch owners brought tourists out for a look. It seemed everyone was curious about the crazy gringos and their strange house.

As Mercedes and I scraped the barrel for the last drops of acrylic and mixed the last batch for Joe to spread, I looked out and saw the familiar shape of the Wilsons' boat heading in our direction.

We could make out Mario's form standing behind Len and directing him around hidden boulders. Many of the dugouts around our island swiftly disappeared as the motor boat sped around *El Corazón* and stopped at our sheltered dock.

"My, my," Mr. Wilson commented as he strode by me. "Looks like some dern cathedral, it does!" He stepped back and stared at the roof. Mario went through exactly the same motions.

Joe finished spreading the last of the acrylic and jumped down. "Howdy, neighbor," he said with his hillbilly drawl. "What'cha think about this newfangled roofing system?"

Mr. Wilson removed his cap and scratched his head. Mario did, too. "I don't really know what to think until I see what happens in the rain," he answered. He walked underneath and looked up. "It's mighty hot in here, isn't it?"

Joe was busy taking down scaffolding, and I tried to busy myself in the kitchen. "Well, sir," I could hear Joe say, "once it's painted white it will reflect the sun and be cooler than it is now."

Len chuckled. Mario chuckled. "I hope you're right about that!"

"Pull up a stool and sit a while," I called, and he came around the plum tree and into our kitchen. "How's Bea?"

"She's not too well," Len answered. "I think her sugar level is messed up."

"Why don't you two come for lunch this Sunday," I offered. "Maybe she'll be feeling better by then, and it will give her a break."

"Have you two been listening to the VOA?" Mr. Wilson asked.

"Not too much," I answered. "We found another station we like better. Did you ever hear of HCJB out of Quito, Ecuador?"

"No, and don't want to," he said. "Batteries cost too much to listen to the radio for entertainment. It's strictly news for us and no more!"

I just kept scrubbing our vegetables.

"Anyway," he continued, "the country's going to pot! Some peanut farmer from Georgia is running for president! Can you imagine? I never even heard of him."

"You know it's terrible," I said, "but I'd forgotten about the elections."

"You may as well forget about the United States!" Len stated adamantly. "I'm glad we got out when we did, and you will be, too!"

When I made no comment, he and Mario stood up to leave.

"I hope you can come for Sunday dinner," I said once more. "I'll be expecting you unless I hear otherwise."

Joe and I walked them down to the dock and waved good-by. When I told Joe what Len had said about the U.S., he just shrugged and said, "Poor fellow! He must have had a hard time. I'm just glad he and Bea have found a place they can call home."

There was a check for ten dollars from my mother-in-law's friends in the Pilot Club. The note said they were sorry about the belated gift.

We were thrilled! That was the equivalent of seventy dollars in Nicaragua. We could pay for our sand and tile to be delivered!

That night we began a tape to mail home. It felt as if we were talking on the phone to our families about all that had happened in the last few days. I couldn't wait for them to come to visit us and see our little place. I drew maps showing the location of the island compared to the peninsula and other islands. Then I tried to sketch the location of everything on the island.

The next morning I planted a garden. Now that the house was far enough along so the area wouldn't be trampled, I cleared a little eight-by twenty-foot spot of ground and tried to break up the rocky soil with the steel bar. Though my hands were raw by noon, I was pleased with my progress.

I put some potatoes in the oven to bake and had just gone back to the garden when I heard a cracking sound. Joe was up on a homemade ladder painting, and I glanced up to see him falling from the roof down to the rocks below.

He seemed to move in slow motion. Unable to help him, I stood frozen as he landed in a crumpled heap. As I ran to him, he looked up and moaned.

Mercedes wasn't working with us that day, and I didn't know what to do. I couldn't even move Joe by myself, much less get him into the boat.

"Oh, Lord," I cried, "please help me."

At that moment I looked up and saw one of Mercedes' children rowing toward the island with a fish for Cory.

"*Ayudame, por favor!*" I cried out. I told her to tell Mercedes what had happened.

By that time, Joe was dusting himself off and saying he was all right. But he had a bleeding gash in his side.

"No!" I yelled at him. "You're going to a doctor. What if you have internal injuries? What would I do in the middle of the night if you needed to be checked? There's no way I'm taking a chance on that. We're going!"

He tried to get up and moaned as he stood. "Okay," he agreed, "but I really think I'm fine."

I looked up at the broken board twelve feet above us on the ladder. "Look how far you fell!"

He glanced up and limped toward the steps. I didn't even bother to change clothes or put on a skirt.

When we got to the dock in Asese, Joe felt a little nauseous and was glad we had come.

I drove to the Granada hospital, a run-down, Spanish-style building. There was no emergency entrance, so I drove the truck up to the front doors and jumped out. Several nuns walked out, stared at my attire, and walked on as if I wasn't there.

Joe stepped cautiously down from the seat of the truck. Several people stared at him, but none offered to help. I already regretted not having taken the time to change.

I ran in and started asking questions about where to take Joe for some attention. Everyone I talked with gave me a puzzled look and shook his head.

"I don't know what's going on!" I said to Joe as I walked out to where he was leaning against the truck. "Nobody seems interested in helping us."

He stopped a young man leaving the hospital and explained to him what had happened. The fellow looked at us with a puzzled expression and asked why we weren't at the doctor's.

"The doctor's?" we asked in unison.

"*Sí!*" the young man answered and explained we needed to go to the doctor's home for attention, not the hospital!

We didn't understand, but we drove a few blocks to the home of a doctor we had heard the Wilsons mention. Dr. Barquero was Bea's doctor.

A young woman answered the door and ushered us quickly through a beautifully landscaped courtyard to the office area of the home. The doctor introduced himself, and to our surprise he spoke fluent English. He had attended medical school in the United States!

He gave Joe a thorough examination. Once the gash in his side was cleaned, it was obvious it wouldn't require any stitches. "He's bruised and will need to take it easy for a few days," the doctor said. "Otherwise, he's going to be good as new."

I was so relieved and grateful to know a doctor if we ever needed one again. He asked us many questions about why we were living on the island, why we had come to Nicaragua, and what our plans were once we finished building the house. We tried to satisfy his curiosity, but I could tell he wondered why a young couple from the United States would want to make their new home in Nicaragua.

As we got up to go I asked him how much we owed him for his services. He looked at us and smiled. I was a little anxious as I realized how much of his time we had taken.

"That will be twenty-eight cordobas," he said, "unless that seems too much."

Four dollars! I couldn't believe my ears. We paid him and assured him we would always call on him whenever we needed a doctor.

As we drove back to Asese we passed the slaughterhouse, the market, and the same old dirty houses, but for the first time, I wasn't repulsed. It felt like home.

The next morning the tile and sand were delivered on one of the tourist launches. Days earlier we had arranged for a man to come and "install" the new tile floor. I couldn't imagine how a floor would be installed on dirt, but I was about to find out.

The fellow who jumped off the launch looked just like Mick Jagger of the Rolling Stones. With him was a young man who carried all the tools.

Mercedes was rowing as quickly as he could toward the island. In no way was he going to miss out on this new experience. It was a good thing he had come because Joe wasn't in very good shape to help carry the heavy stacks of clay tile up from the dock to the house.

We had raked and cleaned the dirt underneath our new roof for days. Using a four-foot level, we'd tried to prepare the ground for the tile. As soon as the tiles were unloaded, the tile-layer squatted down in one corner of our house and began work. Using a mixture prepared by his helper, he spread cement right onto the dirt for an area about the size of four tiles. Then he used a rubber mallet to tap the twelve-inch squares into place. By the end of the day, half our house had a real floor.

It looked so different as we peered through the beams to the other side. Cory scampered to our side, stopped in her tracks, and stared at the odd-looking surface in front of her. Cautiously she stretched her paw in front of her and touched the cool tile. Then she stepped onto it with her front feet and walked gingerly across it to lie down in the middle of what would soon be our bedroom. She rolled over and pawed the air and then jumped up and ran to the other side. Whatever this new floor was, she liked it!

We laughed at our curious cat. "Her little world has changed in a few short months," I said to Joe as he hugged me close.

"And so has ours!" he laughed. We began to chase each other around the island and ended up jumping into the lake from the dock.

"Oh!" I shouted, looking to the west. Joe turned to see what I was so excited about. The sky had turned a dozen shades of coral as the sun slipped behind Mombacho.

We pulled ourselves up onto the rocks and sat down. Joe hugged me close. We watched the sky for several minutes, and spontaneously both of us began to clap and shout "bravo" as if we had just heard the finest symphony in the world.

"Wow!" I whispered. "This must be how Adam and Eve felt before they disobeyed God."

Joe kept staring at the extraordinary hues in the western sky and softly began to sing the opening line of "How Great Thou Art." I joined him as he started the chorus: "Then sings my soul. . . ."

When we finished singing, we stared at the countless stars above us. I couldn't believe the peace that swept over me. Joe took me in his arms, and we became one with God's universe.

SIXTEEN

When the Rains Come

We were up bright and early the next morning. About 7:30 we could see the red and white launch delivering our workmen. They worked all day and were done by five that afternoon. We paid them, and after final instructions on how to care for the floor and how long to wait before walking on it, they left.

"Now we can start on the louvered panels for the walls," Joe said as he walked the perimeter of the house and inspected the floor.

The next morning we drove into town for supplies and to order the lumber for our walls.

We had a package at the post office, and I eagerly tore it open. Inside was an empty milk jug, two empty egg cartons, shorts for Joe, and a bucket of peanut butter! Our families had heard our tapes and knew our needs.

As we drove around the park toward the market I noticed a huge crowd of people gathered outside a new store. Joe pulled over and let me out. When I asked several people on the crowded sidewalk what was going on, they answered, "*Supermercado!*"

A supermarket for Granada? I hoped they were right. I had become accustomed to the marketplace crowds and pushed my way through just like any other Nicaraguan. Near the front I could see a couple of young boys unveiling a newly painted sign: *Supermercado Lacayo*. I stumbled back through the crowd and told Joe the news.

"You'll still need to shop in the market, you know." he said. "I'd say their prices will be just as high as Managua."

"Well, I want to find out for myself," I announced.

Joe parked the truck in front of a hardware store, and I made my way back around the block to the new supermarket.

The first thing I noticed inside was the air conditioning. This was the first building I'd entered in Granada that was artificially cooled. With the high ceilings and electric fans, most places didn't need it.

I walked in and passed the service desk, where several women were leaving their shopping bags and purses with a young girl. I had left my basket in the truck and only had my shopping list, so I strolled by without stopping. Suddenly I heard the familiar "Ch, Ch, Ch" that was the way Nicaraguans got someone's attention. I turned to see the girl was motioning me toward her.

I walked over and spoke, but she stared at my shopping list. *"No puedes entrar con esa!"* she said, indicating that I could not enter with my list.

"Como?" I asked in disbelief. I explained I had to have my list or I wouldn't know what to buy, but she insisted that she had been instructed to take everything and keep it until shoppers left the store.

I couldn't believe my ears. Surely the store manager didn't intend for this employee to interpret the instructions so literally.

I looked around and finally saw a young woman who appeared to be in charge. I motioned for her to assist me, and she graciously listened as I explained what was happening.

She started laughing and told me to go on—with my list! When I looked back, the young girl behind the service desk was listening patiently as the manager kindly explained her instructions once more.

I walked up and down the aisles and saw several things I had been unable to buy in the native market. Some things were cheaper, but a lot of items were much higher. I made notes on my list and then went to the meat department. It was a joy to see. The beef was kept cold, and the prices were written for all to see.

Those were two things I'd never grown accustomed to in the market— seeing the hanging strips of meat and asking the price every time I bought any, never knowing if I was getting the best price of the day or not.

As I made my way around the store I noticed young women standing at each end of every aisle. Something else caught my attention: large jars of mayonnaise and other items on one aisle, medium-sized jars on another, and the smaller jars on another—all of the same product!

I wondered what kind of system could possibly be used in stocking the store, but didn't find out until later when I asked about Kool-Aid.

I was directed to the makeup and toiletries section of the supermarket. I thought at first they must have misunderstood me, but sure enough, there was the Kool-Aid right alongside the lipstick.

I couldn't contain my curiosity any longer, so I again went to the manager and asked the reason for the arrangement of products.

She looked at me curiously and patiently explained their system to me. All the items in the store were placed together according to size. Since Kool-Aid is very little and can be stolen more easily, it is placed with the little cosmetic items where it must be paid for in that area of the store. The women at either end of the aisles were also there to be sure no one was stealing.

My eyes must have been as big as saucers as I listened to her explanation. I couldn't believe there could be that big a problem with theft! Joe and I had never once worried about having anything stolen since we'd been in Nicaragua. I thanked her for her time with me and walked to the check-out with a few items.

They had obviously never heard of an express lane, and I waited for a long time to pay for fewer than ten items.

On the way back to the island I explained the supermarket's stocking procedures to Joe. He laughed and laughed. We had both worked in grocery stores as teenagers and couldn't help comparing the differences.

In the afternoon, we could see the sky getting darker and darker in the northeast. The rumble of thunder rolled across the sky as a calm settled on the island. Even the birds were quiet. We watched hundreds of huge, white herons soar past on their way to roost on another island during the storm.

We hurried around trying to be sure everything was tied down, closed up, or stored away before the rains came.

Joe was especially anxious since this would be the first rain on the new roof. He chattered nervously about the acrylic coating and whether or not we had used the correct paint. He hadn't been able to finish painting since his accident and that worried him.

"We'll find out soon enough!" I said as the wind began to blow, picking up the waves and crashing them on the eastern end of the island.

"Is everything ready?" Joe asked as he glanced around our campsite one more time. He ran to get us something to drink from the refrigerator and then ducked into the tent as the first drops pelted the tent.

Lightning flashed all around us and the tent leaned with the wind. We lay there in silence with Cory curled at our feet and watched the yellow roof for leaks. Cory's loud purring harmonized with the pelting raindrops. Suddenly, I heard a trickle of water on the floor of our tent. I leaned over Joe and peered at the floor. Right at the base of the zippered flap a little river was spilling in.

"I'll go dig a trench to reroute it." Joe swung his legs down from our plywood bed.

"Hey," I insisted, "let me! I've got my rain gear we bought in Corpus Christi, and this is the perfect time to try it out!"

"Are you sure?" Joe asked incredulously.

I was already up pulling on my coat and pants. I stepped from the tent. The rain beat down on my back as I ran for the shovel, came back to the tent, and dug furiously. My efforts paid off immediately. The little river of water flowed away from the tent and down through the rocks. I started singing at the top of my lungs as if I could drown out the sound of thunder. "Shall we gather at the river. . . ."

When the storm blew over, I glanced around the island. Again, every leaf glistened. The roof of our new house was steaming, and I rushed to look in and see how the floor looked. Our new tile floor looked freshly waxed. The rain had blown through the house and polished the tiles to a high sheen.

Joe emerged from the tent with Cory at his heels. He hurried over to the house and looked in. "Well, can't tell if the roof leaks from the looks of this!"

We walked around cautiously. Most of the water was pouring from the perimeter of the roof as it was supposed to do, but we spotted a few drops of water coming through the newly coated screen in several places.

"I saved a little of the mixture for that purpose," Joe said to reassure me in case I was beginning to doubt our roofing system.

"Well, that's okay," I said. "It's not like we have these storms all day long. In this weather who cares about a few leaks anyway!"

Joe looked at me and grinned. "What a woman!"

I checked the tent, and everything seemed to be dry. But later that afternoon I returned to the tent to unpack some pots and pans that I had never used. As I dug under the board where we stored our clothes, my hand felt wetness. I unstacked the clothing and discovered the tent wasn't doing as well as I had thought.

Everything that touched the outer wall of the tent was soaked. One of the new pots was full of water, and sitting right in the middle of the whole mess was Joe's thirty-five millimeter camera. As I pulled it out of the water, I realized I didn't know if it had gotten wet from this rain or the one a few days before. I dreaded telling Joe, but knew I had to. I stepped from the tent and called for him.

He looked up from where he was measuring the floor of the house. "What is it?"

I held up the dripping camera.

"What in the world happened?" Joe exclaimed as he ran to me and grabbed the camera.

He looked through the viewer and let out a gasp. "Look through it!" he groaned. When I did, all I could see was water jiggling inside the lens.

"Maybe if we set it on a rock the hot sun will dry it out," I offered consolingly.

"We'll have to try it," he said, removing the lens and opening the camera.

I looked in at the clean tile floor of the house. "Joe, do you think we could move the tent into the house until we're finished?"

He looked up and stared ahead for a few minutes, thinking. "I don't see why not," he answered.

"All right!" I cried with enthusiasm. "In the morning we move!"

The next day was beautiful. While Joe cut, planed, and built the louvered panel that would soon be our bathroom window, I cleaned the tent and aired out our things. That day I washed more than one hundred articles of rain-soaked clothing that had begun to mildew.

Even so, by the end of the day the tent was moved into the house and Joe had the bathroom walls finished.

We fell into bed exhausted. Cory, who didn't quite understand where her house had been moved, was meowing loudly. But once she saw we were going to sleep just as we always had, she joined us and settled into her contented ball at our feet.

We tuned in to HCJB and continued studying the gospels. We looked forward to that nightly time with each other. After "Unshackled" was over, we turned off the radio and reached for our cassette recorder.

It was Joe's night to emcee our newsletter to our families. We took turns telling of the latest island happenings. Just as Joe was trying to explain about the roof and the latest developments on the house, I spotted some kind of animal as it scurried in the six-inch opening of the zipper where Cory came in and out of the tent.

"What's that?!" I screamed as Cory pounced on the tiny creature from the bed. "Get it, Cory. Get it!" I shouted. She was busy doing her best to capture whatever it was.

Joe and I were up on our hands and knees watching the whole scene. Cory cornered the little creature and grabbed it around the neck. She was hopping around on her back legs and slinging the writhing creature.

"Get it out of here!" I screamed.

Joe and I started laughing at the sight of our sweet little cat turned to ferocious predator. Cory was showing off her skill, not the least bit hungry, for her belly was bulging from the fish we had caught earlier in the evening.

Joe finally grabbed the furry animal from her as she tossed it in the air and slung it outside the tent. Cory then streaked out of the tent like a flash of lightning and was back with it in seconds.

"Throw it in the lake!" I demanded.

"How about if I put it in the refrigerator until tomorrow?" Joe teased me.

"Throw it in the lake!" I insisted again.

Cory was standing straight up, reaching for the little shrew. She was obviously not finished playing, but Joe slung the furry creature in the lake anyway.

Cory ran outside and searched and searched. Finally she came back to the tent and sat at the zipper for a long time scanning the ground. Her whiskers and ears twitched with every sound.

After a while she came back into the tent and hopped up on top of the cassette recorder. We were trying to finish our "letter" home, but she was demanding her petting time regardless.

Ah, the excitement on an island. We hoped our families didn't think we'd gone completely off the deep end as they listened to the tape.

SEVENTEEN

One with God's Children

I had looked forward to the next day for what seemed like an eternity. We were going to town to buy our bathroom fixtures! It seemed like forever since I'd had any privacy, and the potty was breaking down.

As we prepared to leave, Joe stopped and looked around the island. "You know, Sandy," he surveyed all that had been done in the last few months, "God sure has been good to us. The way He helped us pick out our old truck, the way the rains held off until now—just everything."

"It is amazing!" I agreed.

"You know, I was just thinking about what we've been reading in the Bible about giving. He has given us so much we should at least set aside a part of our savings for Him. What do you think?"

"I remember reading something at the last of the Old Testament the other night." I went into the tent to get the Bible.

"Here it is." I flipped to Malachi 3:10. "It says to bring all the tithes into the storehouse, and prove the Lord. He says He will open the windows of heaven, and pour out a blessing, that we shall not have room enough to receive it!"

"That settles it, then," Joe said. "Today we open up a separate account for the Lord's purposes, and we'll promise not to touch it unless it's for His work, okay?"

I thought of all the things we needed for the house. And there still was no sign of a job for either one of us once the money ran out. I was kind of skeptical about tithing the ten percent the Bible spoke of. "How much are you talking about?" I asked.

"I think we should set aside a full ten percent of the amount we came down here with," Joe said as he figured. "We sent five thousand down a year ago for the island and we had five thousand with us when we arrived, so that would be one thousand dollars—seven thousand cordobas!"

"Are you sure, Joe?"

"After what we've been reading and studying, I'd be afraid not to. But that's not the real reason. God has done so much for us. Just imagine if one of us had gotten a terrible sickness here or if the rains had started on time or if the truck or boat motor had blown up. Any of these things could have happened, you know? If we trust God enough to take care of all our things, we should be able to trust His promise about our money, shouldn't we?"

I still wasn't so sure, but Joe's enthusiasm and the promise in Malachi that said "Prove me" made me think it was worth trying. "Okay," I agreed.

We drove to Granada and went straight to the bank. In a separate savings account we set aside the seven thousand cordobas and Joe locked the little bank book in a metal box in the back of the camper. He was so cheerful about the whole transaction, I couldn't help being happy too. Besides, today we were buying a real "potty" that would flush!

The next day was Sunday so we slept in late. The tent was so much more comfortable in the living room of our unfinished house. Our "kitchen" had been blocking all the wind from the tent, and it had become difficult to sleep in the heat. Now, we were in the open again, and the night breezes were wonderful.

I'd grown so accustomed to a dirt floor that my legs hurt from walking around on the tile. It didn't matter, though. Even sweeping would thrill me. After the dirt, the tile was a joy to keep clean.

We hadn't planned to do anything but swim and read and sleep all day, but about noon we saw a launch headed our way.

"Maybe it's just some more tourists coming to see the latest developments by the crazy gringoes," I said as it drew closer.

Joe wiggled into his old orange shorts. Since we'd moved the tent inside the house, he'd enjoyed being able to run around in his "birthday suit."

He looked through the binoculars and handed them to me. "Looks like Americans," I said as I got up and ran to the tent to make the bed.

Within minutes the launch was docking at our rock pier and our visitors jumped out. They were a man and a woman about our parents' ages, and they introduced themselves.

"Mr. and Mrs. Tunnell," the man said as he held out his hand to us. "We're the parents of one of the UT students and heard about you and wanted to come to see how you were doing."

They were a delightful couple, and as we showed them around the island, I noticed she was watching me very closely. After a while, as Mr. Tunnell and Joe were discussing the plans for completion of the house, she drew me aside.

"Are you homesick?" she asked.

Even though I'd just met this woman, her question brought me close to her immediately. She became my substitute mother for that afternoon.

"Oh, I have been," I admitted. "Several times I've wanted to go home and forget the whole crazy idea, but then something has always happened and my love for Joe holds me here."

We talked for hours. It turned out that she, too, had moved far away from her family when she first left home and had also had to adjust to a primitive lifestyle. We laughed over the similarities of our experiences. As we talked I drew strength from her encouragement.

By the time they had left, we felt we'd been with family. They both were returning to Tennessee in just a few days and promised to call our families and tell them about our little island and how we were doing.

"Gosh, it felt good to talk, didn't it?" I commented to Joe as we settled down for a nap.

"Especially with somebody who encourages us instead of complaining all the time," Joe agreed. He was referring to the Wilsons. The woman I'd just met was the same age as Bea yet seemed and looked twenty years younger.

"I hope when I'm older I'll encourage young women to stick with their dreams no matter what. It was such a lift to talk with her."

"He was interesting, too," Joe said. "Funny, if my dad were still alive, we probably would have talked about the same things."

I fixed us a big salad with everything I could find in the refrigerator. I also surprised Joe with a lemon pie that evening.

In the next few weeks we completed the bathroom, and I couldn't even wait until we painted to have my first private bath in six months!

We also finally got our pump working and filled the tank. Our arms were sore for three days from all the pumping. It took 470 pumps to fill our little water tank, and every flush of the toilet used about 25 pumps. After two weeks I got the pumping down to a fine science and didn't pump any more than I needed.

We planned to spend July Fourth in Managua. The students had told us about a huge celebration at the Harvard Business School, and we were eager to celebrate our home nation's independence day with other Americans.

I had been thinking a lot lately about the difference between the United States and Nicaragua. I wondered why a country as young as ours could have progressed so far in many different areas—technology, science, education, housing, agriculture, and others—while one as old as Nicaragua still had such primitive ways. A minority of Nicaraguans lived and worked in the technological age, but the majority we'd seen were still living as if in a pre-industrial century. Was the difference because of the climate, the government, what? The answers eluded me.

As we drove to Managua that Saturday morning, we were excited about meeting the embassy staff, Peace Corps volunteers, and the other Americans who would attend.

When we pulled into the parking lot at the Harvard Business School, we were amazed at how many people were there.

"I had no idea there were this many Americans in Nicaragua," I commented as we pulled "Old Moses" into an empty space between two Mercedes Benz.

Many of the students were there and introduced us to others as "that couple I told you about who live on the island."

We began to feel a little odd as people questioned why in the world we'd *choose* to live in Nicaragua. We certainly got odd expressions as we described the people's warm hospitality, Mercedes and his family, and the wonderful way we'd been treated at government offices and most of the borders.

As soon as possible, we broke away from the questioning crowds and got involved in some games. It was like a fair, and we sprinted from one event to another like little children. We were giggling with excitement.

By the end of the day, we'd eaten our fill of hot dogs and hamburgers and "pigged out" on chocolate chip cookies and potato chips from the U.S.

As the fireworks display lit up the velvet night, Joe and I sat on the hillside in each other's arms with tears streaming down our faces.

"We're blessed, you know?" Joe whispered in my ear.

I nodded in agreement. A spectacular finale with the American flag lit up the field below us, and we stood to our feet and cheered, "God bless America."

We drove back to Mel Eberhard's for the night, with my heart full enough to burst with the day's events. As we climbed into bed I commented to Joe, "Never have I spent a more meaningful Fourth of July. It's as if I'm seeing our country and what it stands for for the first time."

"I guess it's like a lot of things we've experienced this year," Joe agreed. "Maybe doing without things like running water, electric lights, telephones, and television, and especially our families and friends has made us appreciate them more than we ever would have if we'd stayed in Kingsport."

The next day we attended Mel's church and then went to Villa Verona for the students' celebration of the Fourth. By evening I was ready to return to the island. After the tranquil life I'd grown accustomed to, city life was exciting but exhausting.

The next morning we bought our bathroom tile and headed home. As we sped across the water I could already imagine how upset Cory was going to be. Sure enough, she was waiting at the dock, meowing pitifully. She rubbed against our legs, then scampered off and acted like she didn't need us anyway.

That evening I began to feel terrible. My head hurt, and my insides were churning in painful nauseous spasms. I couldn't get comfortable no matter how I sat or lay. About nine o'clock it started. I was never so sick in my life.

Joe had to clean up after me all through the night. "What could it be?" he pleaded aloud.

The only thing I could think of that I had eaten and Joe hadn't was some chicken. "That has to be it!" I moaned. I was in agony.

"We're going to have to get you to a doctor," Joe said at about three o'clock in the morning. "I don't know what to do for you."

At that moment I didn't even care if I lived. Every few minutes I would fall toward the potty. I couldn't make it outside the tent.

Joe was nervous. He didn't know how to help me, and he didn't want to chance making it to Asese in the dark. If he damaged the boat, we'd be stuck in the water until morning.

Finally, Joe cried out, "Oh, Lord, help us! Make Sandy well in the name of Jesus Christ!"

I was crying from the excruciating pain. There was nothing left inside me, yet my body kept wrenching itself trying to expel whatever was making me sick. I was wet with perspiration, yet chilling till my teeth chattered.

As Joe cried out, I couldn't even hope there would be an answer to his prayer, but as the minutes passed, miraculously I felt the nausea leaving me and the fever subsiding.

Joe was crying with gratitude. "Thank You, Lord, oh, thank You," he said over and over as I began to drift to sleep.

By morning I was sleeping peacefully, and Joe was anxious for Mercedes to get to work. When he arrived Joe told him of the horrible night I'd had, and Mercedes agreed it must have been the chicken.

About 10:30 that morning, Mercedes rowed home and returned with two tin plates heaped high with rice, beans, and plantano. I was still weak, but the food tasted so good I wolfed it down. Joe appreciated the food as well, and I promised Mercedes that I would bake his family a cake soon.

Day after day we were learning more about the all-caring God we had chosen to serve. Living as we were, we were dependent on His grace and care.

By our seven-month anniversary, July 27, we were well on our way to comfort. We had a real running-water bathroom (although Joe still preferred the lake so he didn't have to pump so much), we were building the cabinets for the kitchen, and it wouldn't be long before we had the frame built for our water-bed.

Joe placed seven tiny orchids in a bowl on our crude wooden dinner table that afternoon. As we sat down to eat in our tarp-roofed hut, we looked into each other's eyes. His bright green eyes had a sparkle I'd not noticed, and he said the same about mine.

"You've come a long way, baby!" he said as he took my hand and asked

the blessing for our food. We now realized the importance of God's blessing on the food we ate. In fact, many things we'd taken for granted just
months earlier were now precious.

As we finished eating, the Wilsons' boat appeared making its way toward our island. It was late in the day for them to venture away from
home, and I wondered if something was wrong.

We ran down to the dock and greeted them. Even Bea had undertaken
the journey which for her was a great effort.

"What brings you two here?" Joe asked. He also welcomed Mario, in
Spanish.

"Ah, the Mrs. just had to see your progress," Len chuckled. "Now, we
can't stay but a few minutes 'cause it's almost time for the VOA and we'll
have to be back home for that."

I was happy to show her Joe's handiwork, and she gaped at everything
as I explained how the roof worked and showed her our little corner
bathroom.

She wheezed with every step, but was determined to see everything.
She hobbled slowly around the island and after commenting, "You sure
have done a lot of work!" she headed back toward the steps where Len
and Joe were talking.

"I wish you could stay a little longer," I said. But they insisted on leaving so we waved good-by and watched them pull away. They had found
no basis for a quarrel on this inspection.

It rained all night, but the next morning was beautiful and sunny. "I
guess the rainy season is definitely upon us," I commented as Joe checked
the roof for leaks and began working on another louvered wall panel.

"Yeah," he agreed, "and the paint we used is starting to concern me.
It's cracking in places! I hope it doesn't pull the coating with it!"

Sure enough, tiny cracks were showing up on our beautiful, screen
roof. I didn't even want to think about what we would do with a leaky
roof. So I unpacked some wedding gifts to keep my mind off the possibility of a rain-soaked house.

I made a cake for another island family and decided I'd get some exercise by rowing it over on our raft. I put the cake down in the cooler, and
Joe helped me get situated so I could row with my arms.

He was laughing as I floated away from the dock. "Well, if you get lost at sea, at least you'll have food," he shouted as I maneuvered around the island.

It was a lot farther than I had thought, and I just about gave up as I dug my arms into the water again and again. I hadn't thought about the sharks in the lake for weeks, but that old fear crept deeper into my consciousness with every stroke into the dark green water. "Fear not!" I heard that now familiar inner voice command. Just as quickly an old song from childhood came to my lips, so I began to sing as I rowed, "Michael, row the boat ashore, hallelujah. . . ."

In no time, I reached my destination. The native family from whom we had purchased *El Corazón* had several teenaged children, and they were staring at me as if they'd just seen a ghost.

I floated alongside a big boulder and cautiously set the cooler on it and then rolled into the water and crawled up on the flat rock.

By this time the whole family was gawking at the crazy gringa and her red and blue box. When I pulled the chocolate cake from inside, they all let out a big "Ah-h-h-h!" and began talking at once.

They appreciated it all right! Señora Carillo insisted on showing me around their island to point out the items they'd purchased with the money from the sale of *El Corazón*. She was especially proud of her new cooking pots and a table with chairs. Then, her two sons ducked into the crude wooden hut and brought out a portable radio with earphones! Their daughter showed me a mirror and new brush and comb with makeup. They were all giggling with excitement over their new "toys."

As I turned to go, their father motioned for me to come look underneath a piece of heavy canvas. As he lifted the material, his face was beaming with pride. No wonder! It was a new five-horsepower boat motor. He clucked his tongue, covered his mouth with his hand, and chuckled like a little child. Then he motioned for me to look at something else, a new kerosene lantern.

"You've got everything, don't you?" I asked hoping they would understand my Spanish. They laughed and nodded their heads as I left. They kept calling out *"Gracias!"* as I rowed out of sight.

It took a while to get back to *El Corazón*. Joe was still working as I rowed by. "Hey, you up there!" I yelled. "You need good woman?"

He laid down the saw and hurried to the edge of the water. Before I could row away, he had dumped me off the raft, and I grabbed the cooler and swam on to the dock.

As Joe chased after me, I suddenly realized the dream of two brown, beautiful people enjoying God's creation in our own little paradise was coming true!

By our eight-month anniversary, August 27, we were sleeping in our water bed under the new roof! I couldn't believe how comfortable it was. It took me several mornings to break the habit of stooping over to dress as I had in the tent.

Cory jumped up on the bed after finding we weren't in the tent. Barely had her paws touched the wiggling bed when she meowed loudly and shot off the strange new addition to the house.

"Poor little Cory!" I laughed. "You're not about to get near water if you can help it, are you?"

Joe picked her up and tossed her onto the bed anyway. She darted off again. I had secretly hoped she would stay away from it because of her claws, and it looked like she was determined to dislike it. But that night as we climbed in, she stepped cautiously onto the buoyant bed. By the end of our radio programs, she was resting comfortably as usual in a curl at our feet.

"Oh, well," Joe said, "some things are just more important to a cat than fear of water."

By the end of August, we were running low on money and starting to wonder what we would do for jobs. We checked on several possibilities including perhaps developing another island for tourism and working with UT students in Granada, but nothing was working out.

I wrote in my diary:

> We've made it through all this! Now with bathroom, kitchen and "almost" walls around, life is so much more enjoyable for those of us from a civilized existence. We love it here! Our peaceful and wonderful feeling of accomplishment needs only our families to share it with. Oh, how I want them to see God's handiwork here and see life from a different direction that they may appreciate the simple luxuries at home.
>
> Thank you, Lord—You've made it all happen. Help us to allow your light and love to show through us.

September was a month of trials. There was still no job prospect for either one of us, and our money supply was too low for us to buy any more materials for the house.

"Shouldn't we just get that money out of that other account?" I asked Joe, referring to our tithe.

"No way," Joe insisted. "God's not failed us yet, and I refuse to believe something won't open up soon."

The days passed slowly. We read a lot of books that the UT students had loaned us and enjoyed visits from big groups of them.

I became increasingly homesick. It was only September, but I knew how soon Christmas would be here. If we had no jobs, there would be no trip home. I thought I'd die if I couldn't see my family, I hadn't seen them in so long. "Trust!" I heard that inner voice say as my mind ran away with the blues.

I recalled reading something a few nights earlier about how God clothes the flowers of the field and the birds of the air. I looked around me at the full flowering trees and the parrots that flew overhead. *If He cares for them that much, surely He cares for me!* I thought. *It's silly to worry about something so far away. If He made the world in seven days, He can get us a job when we need one!* And so my mind was at peace once more.

September was almost over, and quite a bit remained to do on the house. We still had to build a deck, buy some furniture, and have enough money left to go home for Christmas!

"Trust!"

"Okay, okay," I agreed, "I'll trust, but I hope something happens soon, or we'll be fishing for our suppers."

That weekend we decided it was as good a time as any to give Mercedes' family a treat. We rowed and swam over with our homemade raft to see what they thought about heading for the coast.

The children scampered down the rocky cliff and giggled at the sight of us. Rosa Elena looked down from above and her big, round tummy shook with laughter. Mercedes was pulling a shirt on as he came to meet us.

At the mention of San Juan del Sur, a small fishing village about an hour away, Mercedes eyes lit up. Of course he wanted to go—*and* his family? He was astounded that we would ask them. They had never seen the ocean before, and the children were overjoyed.

After conferring with Rosa Elena, Mercedes asked if we could wait one more week. There was no reason not to, so it was agreed. The first weekend of October we would go to the ocean and have a day on the beach!

At least we had that to look forward to during the week that followed. Despite many phone calls and trips to town searching for a job, we had no prospects by the next Saturday. We were both getting depressed.

But our depression evaporated as we stopped to pick up some of the children and hook the dugout with Mercedes and the rest behind our boat. We looked like a jungle safari making its way slowly to the dock at Puerto Asese.

Rosa Elena, Mercedes, Joe, and I piled into the front of the truck with all of the children sitting in the camper behind. We bounced along the road heading south.

Rosa Elena was wearing a new handmade apron, and she had made each of the children a playsuit of cotton material with safety pins for buttons. Mercedes had on a new pair of pants—at least we'd never seen him wearing them before. They were obviously used, but they had no patches. He also wore a pleated cotton shirt we hadn't seen before.

Obviously this was a very special occasion for this native family. Rosa Elena and I had packed a picnic lunch for all of us. She said she'd prepared *ensalada con yucca* which was one of Joe's and my favorite foods in Nicaragua—shredded cabbage and yucca root with a hot vinegar sauce served with *chicharrón*—fried pork skin with chunks of meat still attached.

I'd made potato salad and macaroni salad along with a cake and some cookies. Mercedes had insisted on buying a whole case of soft drinks, so we were definitely going to have a feast.

When we pulled onto the beach at San Juan del Sur, the children piled out of the camper and squinted into the bright sun toward the ocean.

They waited until Mercedes motioned that it was all right to go on into the water, and then they took off toward the crashing waves. As they bent down into the water to scoop up a drink, they made faces and screamed "It's salty!" and ran to show their mama.

Joe and I realized these children had no idea what the ocean was going to be like. They had never been to school and rarely been to town. Since they could neither read nor write, how could they have known?

Mercedes began shedding his clothes. He had on a beautifully flowered swimsuit—at least that's what we thought until the first wave crashed into him. Then, his flowered swimsuit came apart. A blue-flowered hand towel floated onto the beach. I was afraid to look at first, but then Joe assured me he had on underwear. Mercedes ran onto the beach, tried to fix the towel back in place, then gave up and just went on swimming anyway.

Rosa Elena sat on a blanket and giggled until I thought she'd never stop at the sight of her husband and children. We sat together on the beach to eat lunch. The children had never seen macaroni before and dutifully tasted my salad. Obviously, all of us enjoyed Rosa Elena's dish much more than mine and I marked off macaroni salad for all future picnics with the island people.

After eating we went exploring. The children had no shoes of course and made their way like little mountain goats over the sharp, jagged edges of the black rock along the coast. I felt like a big baby as I whined with every step until one of the children ran back to get my tennis shoes. I couldn't thank her enough as I caught up with the others.

Waves were crashing along the shore and spraying us as we climbed. Around a corner, we spotted an old fishing vessel broken to pieces on the rocks. The kids climbed in and out of the wreckage and found all kinds of sea life that they picked up without hesitation and brought to us to identify. We recognized many of the creatures but had no idea of their Spanish names.

Every once in a while they would bend down and scoop up some water in their palms, touch their tongues to it, and gag. Then they would giggle and splash away. It was a joy to see their innocence and enthusiasm.

The day was over too quickly. As the sun headed to the west, we had to leave in order to get back to the island before dark.

The children splashed and played while we loaded up our empty bottles and picnic supplies. Then Mercedes whistled, and they came running to climb into the back of the truck. As they all got seated I looked at their beaming faces and felt as if I'd just given someone the dream of his life.

When we arrived back at Puerto Asese, half the children were sound asleep. We loaded them all into the boat and the dugout and slowly motored home. A dark cloud passed over just as we approached Mercedes' island and a few drops of rain washed the salt from our bodies.

As we helped them unload, Mercedes came toward Joe and grabbed his arm with a firm handshake. *"Gracias, amigo, muchas gracias!"* I believe I saw a tear in his eye as he turned to carry one of the children up to the little hut. We called, *"Buenos noches,"* as we pulled away.

"I'm so glad we were able to do that with them," I commented to Joe as we docked the boat at our island.

"Me, too," Joe agreed. "I'll never forget the looks on those children's faces."

The next week we piddled around trying to figure out things we could do to complete the house without money. We built a few shelves in the bathroom and cleaned up the island of fallen palm branches. There just wasn't much we could do without materials.

A fellow we'd met at the Fourth of July picnic and his wife came to see us. He was employed by the Harvard Business School, and it turned out we had mutual acquaintances in Kingsport.

He encouraged us to introduce ourselves to the president of Granada's Chamber of Commerce, David Callejas. "Perhaps he can help you two find employment."

The next day we dressed neatly and went into Granada. We found David Callejas at his home where he also operated a jelly factory making food products from the guava fruit.

He and his wife Anna had two sons and were expecting another child. They listened with interest as we told them why we had come to Nicaragua and how we loved the islands.

David had attended school in the States and spoke fluent English. Anna understood only Spanish, and as I told them of those first few months on the island, she kept asking why I did things like shopping, washing, and cooking. "Why did you not hire a maid?" she asked.

I couldn't believe it! Joe and I both laughed and commented, "How could we afford that?"

Then she explained how much a maid earned and that in Nicaragua that kind of work isn't done by "our class" of people. As she talked about the class differences and who was responsible for what work in her country, I realized why I had gotten a lot of stares and had been misunderstood many times. No wonder Mercedes had been amazed when I had joined in with the house construction. And Rosa Elena! No wonder she had assumed I wanted her to do my laundry that time I had motioned for her to come for a visit! For the first time those things made sense.

When I thought of Rosa Elena and Mercedes and how much their simple lifestyle had influenced us, how content they were, and how hard they worked every day for the bare minimum of comfort, I knew I could never think of myself as better than they. And besides, what would I have done all day long if I'd had a maid? I laughed at the thought of it.

David and Anna were gracious hosts and invited us to eat lunch with them. The oldest child came home from school, and we all sat down for the noon meal.

"Right offhand I don't know of anywhere to tell you to look for work," David said as we shared their meal, "but I will keep my ears open, and if I hear of anything I'll be sure to let you know."

After lunch, Anna showed me their beautiful home. They too had had their house built according to their plans, but she laughed as I told her how Joe and I had done practically all the work on ours by ourselves with Mercedes' help.

"No puedo creerlo!" she commented. She really couldn't believe it.

We said good-by and drove back to Asese just as a driving rain came sweeping across the lake. "You want to wait it out or go on?" Joe asked as we peered through the sheets of rain between us and the water.

"Oh, let's go on," I insisted. "This could last all night."

So we ran to the boat and jumped in. I was already drenched as we took off across the water. As we increased our speed, the windshield blocked the rain, and we realized for the first time that we could stay dry as long as we were moving. We still were learning. And we had so much yet to learn.

The next weekend Mercedes invited us to another picnic. He and his family came toward the island in a brand new, bright blue and red dugout.

For several weeks, I had been trying to teach him the letters of the Spanish alphabet. He wanted to learn to read, and I knew if he learned, he would go home and teach eight others.

Joe and I had bought some writing tablets and pencils with crayons. Mercedes and his family had never had such things, and he built a special box to store them in.

One afternoon he was bugging me about Tennessee. He wanted to know everything about it. Joe and I tried to describe the beautiful Smoky Mountains, the lakes, and the seasons. Mercedes was fascinated by the thought of a frozen lake. Ice was such a luxury to these island people that he couldn't imagine a whole lake full. Then he had insisted on my showing him how to write the word Tennessee. I couldn't imagine why he wanted that. He had just learned how to write his name! What need could he have to write our state's name?

As he and his family came closer to *El Corazón,* he began to wave excitedly. I glanced around in the waters expecting to see some big fish or something, but he called out, *"Miren, miren aquí!"*

"What does he want us to see?" I asked. Joe and I stared at him and his family filling the huge dugout.

"I don't know," Joe answered, "but he's pretty excited about something. He surely remembers he's already told us about his dugout."

We continued to stare at them as they plowed through the water. As he came alongside our island, he suddenly swung the dugout sideways in the water, and all the children pointed at the side of the boat.

Our eyes filled with tears. Written in bright red letters on the bow of his prize possession was the word *TENNESSEE.* Mercedes had christened his family's boat after our home state. What an honor! And what did it matter that he had written the s's backward? We had never felt so proud.

We piled in with them after hugs and expressions of gratitude. The children grew very quiet as Mercedes explained about the baseball game to be played that afternoon. I couldn't imagine there being enough men to have two teams. We just hadn't seen that many other islanders besides Mercedes' family, the family from whom we had bought the island, and Mario's family. There were a few others we had seen at the dock sometimes, but mostly I had only met the women and young girls as they fished.

But when we arrived at the cleared area on the peninsula, the place was crowded with all people of all ages. The women had swept clean an area beside the baseball field under some trees. There was food everywhere. Joe and I had brought two blocks of ice in the cooler, and I began to chip it up for cups. Everyone was anxious to receive a big plastic cup full of soft drink. Few of these people could afford the luxury of real drinking vessels, and most of them drank from dried gourds. They would use these cups for as long as possible.

Children were everywhere. They were all clean and dressed in the best they had, although their best was an odd collection of worn-out dresses and shorts. Only a very few wore shoes, and I noticed it was mostly the older children in each family.

We were introduced to so many new people I couldn't possibly remember them all. They were rather shy as I tried to communicate my love for them and their islands.

Joe was quickly assigned to Mercedes' team, and the game began. Mercedes was pitcher and showed off the new baseball glove that Joe had given him upon our arrival to Nicaragua.

There was intense competition, but finally, late in the afternoon, the other team won five to four. I could tell Mercedes was very disappointed, but he recovered quickly as we all shared the food.

It was getting dark as we left the picnic. Mercedes bragged that he could find his way around the islands blindfolded. I didn't doubt it one bit as he deftly steered the dugout past boulders beneath the breaking waves and got us home safely.

"You know, Sandy," Joe said as we got ready for bed, "of all the people we've met in Nicaragua and all the beautiful homes we've been in, I still find the island people to be the most loving, genuine folks of the whole nation."

"You're not just a little bit prejudiced?" I laughed. "I don't believe we've met anyone who didn't have a genuine desire to make us feel welcome! All sorts of people from all walks of life have opened their arms and homes to us. I love these people, and today I felt accepted as one of them."

EIGHTEEN

Trusting God's Promise

The following Monday, we had a surprise visitor. A young man came out on a launch and asked if he could interview us for the national newspaper, *La Prensa*.

"What exactly do you want to know about us?" Joe questioned him.

The young man, who looked about our age, introduced himself. He spoke beautiful English with a British accent. "Pardon me," he said. "In my enthusiasm I've forgotten my manners. I'm Pedro Chamorro, an editor for *La Prensa*. I heard about you from a fellow who works with the Harvard Business School."

"Oh, yes," we said. "He told us he'd try to help us find a job. But neither one of us knows anything about the newspaper business!"

"No, no," he chuckled. "I'd like to write a human interest story. It's not every day that a couple from the United States chooses to make Nicaragua their home. I want to know why and how you decided that!"

"First," I interrupted, "please tell us where you learned such beautiful English."

He blushed as he explained that he had gone to school in Canada. He told us a little more about himself, and we discovered that we both had been married on the same date. His wife was expecting a baby at any time, and he invited us to come to Managua sometime to meet her and the rest of his family.

We answered all his questions and showed him all around the island. He took several pictures including one of me pumping water, Joe pretending to do some work, and Cory swinging with us in the hammock.

As he left, we insisted he come visit us again. He assured us he would since his family owned an island on the other side of the peninsula.

We waved good-by and were kind of excited about the possibility of a story about us in the paper.

"You never know, though," Joe contemplated. "He may just be a struggling editor, and the story will never get published. We may as well forget it."

"Besides," I added, "we don't get the paper anyway, so how will we ever know if it's in there or not."

The next morning we planned a new strategy for finding work. Since we'd had no success in Granada, we decided we'd have to look in Managua.

We felt we'd been given the run-around for weeks. We had great ideas and dreams for an island only two miles away that was owned by the Department of Tourism. It was an ideal spot for a park and swimming facilities for the public. Nicaragua had so many fantastic recreational areas but nothing to direct the public to them. Even the cities of the country were unmarked so travelers had to follow a map to figure out where they were.

"We've just got to trust God to open doors for us and give us wisdom to do what we should," I commented to Joe as we waited to talk with a bank officer about our idea.

Finally we were ushered into his office and explained to the man what we were thinking. He was enthused and explained about money available for just such a project. We wrote down all the facts and figures and decided to go back to the island where we could think more about it.

Our money was getting very low. The prospects of borrowing money in order to develop another island didn't really appeal to us since neither of us had steady employment.

The next morning we went to Granada for one last effort to see the mayor about architectural work in the city's planning department. We had been trying to see him for weeks, but he was always out of the office or in meetings.

Surprisingly, he was in and could see us. We felt encouraged as we asked about employment and talked about the possibility of developing the islands for the future. But he gave us no real commitment.

"Doesn't it seem to you," I asked Joe as we left his office, "that lots of people in government here have great enthusiasm for ideas, but always stop short of really committing support to a project?"

"I guess so," Joe said, "but remember we're a couple of gringos, young at that, and they have no idea what we're in the country for anyway. Why should they trust us with a major project like the island development? Maybe someday Nicaragua will realize what it's got to offer the world and do something about it."

We were a little discouraged as we drove back to the island in our motor boat. Dark clouds filled the sky. "Rain's coming," I commented as we passed the island with the dancing children.

Just as we docked at *El Corazón*, the sky opened. As great torrents beat down upon us, we ran for the house and ducked inside. The rain poured off all around the edge of the roof. We had not yet been able to purchase the lumber for our gutters, and it was like sitting behind a waterfall as we watched the rain cascade off the roof.

That evening on HCJB we listened to a drama from the Family Life Institute. It was the story of a family who was in desperate need of a job. The father had been unemployed for months. The mother required hospitalization and their house payment was due in just days.

The family gathered around the table and prayed for God's provision. Incredibly, when the father explained to the bank manager their difficulty in meeting the payment, the manager knew of someone who needed work done. The job was in the father's specialty!

Within hours, the family's needs were met, and we rejoiced with the children as we listened to their grateful thanks to God.

"Surely," Joe said, "something is going to work out for us soon. I really believe what the Bible says about God's provision, and I've also done everything I can to try to find a job, so we're just going to have to trust."

It was a great statement of faith, for in a little sack where I kept our cash were the last seven cordobas we had—our last dollar. I knew better than to bring up "God's account," as we referred to the separate savings account. Joe refused to use that money. I could see his point scripturally, but not practically. After all, didn't God expect us to take care of ourselves first? But every time I brought it up, Joe pointed to a number of verses that proved his viewpoint was the correct one. I wrote in my diary: *"Lord, help my unbelief!"*

The next day dawned sunny and hot. My little garden was yielding yard-long green beans and I went to pick enough for our afternoon meal. Then I looked in the refrigerator and took stock of what we had left.

We had a half dozen eggs, some milk, a little peanut butter in the bucket our parents had sent us, some other vegetables, and a few canned foods.

"Well," I said to Joe, "we won't starve for several more days!"

"We can always fish," Joe commented, trying to laugh, but I knew he was beginning to have his doubts as well.

"What are we going to do today?" I broke the beans into a pot while the day's water supply boiled on the stove.

"I don't know," Joe answered. "I can't think of one place we haven't gone to look for work. I simply refuse to believe that two people like ourselves with college educations can't find work here."

"You wanna help me fish?" I asked.

"Naw," he answered, "go ahead. I've got to do some thinking."

I grabbed our bamboo pole and walked toward the dock. Cory scampered along beside me.

"You think I'm fishing for you, don't you girl?" I asked as Cory rubbed against my leg and meowed. "Well, today it's for Joe and me."

I pulled in two good-sized fish within the next half hour. I was gathering up my "tackle" when I glanced toward Mombacho.

"Looks like we're going to have visitors," I said to Joe as I carried the fish toward the kitchen for cleaning.

"Hey! Looks to me like we're going to have a good supper," he said as he went for the binoculars.

"It's probably just some tourist," he said as he focused in on the launch. "Yep, just some man—never seen him before, but he looks Nicaraguan. Probably wants to see this crazy structure."

But as the launch approached, it slowed and pulled alongside our rocky pier. The man stepped from the launch, holding a newspaper.

"Are you Joe and Sandy?" he asked.

"Why, yes," we answered, but how could he know that?

He opened the newspaper and there on the front page was the headline, "They Found Their Paradise in the Islands." It was an article about us! It continued onto another page complete with pictures. So the young editor had done well and had even gotten on the front page!

As the man realized we hadn't read or even seen the article, he laughed and congratulated us.

"Now, for another surprise," he said. "The man I work for wants to meet you. Can you come with me into Granada?"

We looked at each other and shrugged. "Why not?" we chorused.

"We'll follow you in our boat," Joe said as we ran to change into "town" clothes, a skirt and blouse for me and slacks and shirt for Joe.

The launch owner and the man from Granada stood admiring our project as we wiggled nervously into our clothes. Soon we were speeding across the lake to meet—who knows? It didn't matter. We were both excited about the article and anxious to buy our own copy of *La Prensa* and decipher it for ourselves.

We jumped in our truck and followed the man into Granada. He parked in front of the hardware store.

Some young fellow in a group of students on the corner yelled out, "Joe y Sandy?" We turned as he ran toward us and shook our hands. He and his friends asked so many questions we couldn't understand their rapid-fire Spanish. They even pulled out a paper and asked us to sign it! We were celebrities and didn't know exactly why.

As we entered the cool, dark *ferreteria* the boys behind the counter yelled, "*Bienvenidos*" to us. The man who had come for us led us behind the counter and back through the aisles and aisles of merchandise to a big carved door in the back.

When we entered that door, we felt as though we were in a different building. There were a beautiful conference table, couches, and chairs, and amazingly it was air-conditioned. We sat down, and a young woman entered the room with a fruit drink for both of us.

"What have we done?" I wondered aloud as Joe and I sat there waiting to meet the owner.

"I don't know, but I kinda like it!" Joe said with a laugh.

Within minutes the door opened and a good-looking man walked in. He was about the same height as Joe and wore a beautiful light blue *guayabera*, a pleated shirt, with matching slacks. He smiled the warmest smile we had seen.

"*Hablas en Español?*" he asked first.

We answered, "Yes, we speak a little Spanish."

He introduced himself. "Ramon Lopez, *a la orden.*" He told us he owned and operated four hardware stores, ran a bus service from Granada to Managua and back each day, and also had the distributorship for Mazda in Granada.

Then he produced a copy of *La Prensa* and told us he enjoyed the article very much. He, too, had a dream about his country and had been looking for someone who could help him realize his greatest plans—to develop an attractive hotel and recreational facility for tourists in Granada, his hometown.

Joe and I sat there trying to keep our mouths from gaping open. Talk about answered prayer! We listened to Ramon tell us of his plans.

He wanted to build a huge hotel, complete with swimming pool, spa, and honeymoon suites. He needed an architect to help him design and build the project and someone trained in recreation to help run the facility once it was completed.

We were amazed, but cautious. So many times in the past weeks, we had listened enthusiastically as other people shared their ideas about tourism—but that's all they had done. No one had been really serious or unselfish enough to look toward the future.

When he had finished detailing his plans, he asked us to accompany him to the site of one of his proposed hotels. As we followed him out of the store, Joe and I looked at each other in amazement.

We drove toward the lake and stopped at a beautiful stucco structure sandwiched between other buildings. This was one of Ramon's projects. He had already begun the construction without any architectural drawings, so Joe would need to begin work immediately.

We drove around the lake to another site right on the shores of Lake Nicaragua. Here was a tiny restaurant, but Ramon had plans to expand into a huge motel complex on the beach.

Then we drove toward the peninsula where he pointed out an island he had purchased for development as well! We were flabbergasted. What could we say?

Finally we zoomed around the city and wove in and out of Granada until we arrived across from a cathedral at his residence, a sixteenth-century mansion he had renovated for himself, his wife, and their two children.

He showed us around the home and introduced us to his family. Then we were off again, back to the hardware store and the beautiful conference room where we sat down, breathless.

"Now," he said as he took his wallet from his pocket, "to show you how serious I am, I'm giving you an advance as a deposit on the work I want from you. He held out several hundred cordobas and waited for Joe to take them.

We sat there in disbelief. Before we could even agree or speak, Ramon jerked his head and said, "Oh, and let me show you where your office will be."

We got up and followed him farther back into the building. There was a glassed-in room with a paddle fan. "Here is where we'll put your drawing board, and you will join me and my family for lunch every day. That will be part of your compensation if you agree to work with me. Agreed?"

I was nearly ecstatic. We had no doubts as Joe agreed to come to work—the next day!

As we drove back to Asese and on to *El Corazón* we could hardly speak. God had provided for our needs—in a "tailored" way!

The next morning Joe was up bright and early. I fixed his breakfast, and as he sat down to eat he announced, "I believe I'll water-ski to work."

"What?" I asked. Although we had water-skis, we rarely had the time or the money for gas to use them.

"Yeah! It's not like we're wasting fuel for fun—I've got to go to work. So why not?"

I had to agree, and since he could dress in the truck camper at the dock, there was no reason why he couldn't.

So off we went. I steered carefully through the islands and Joe skied behind. As we passed the dancing children, Joe showed off for them and sent up a spray of water high in the air. They cheered and waved.

I let him out, and we kissed good-by. Suddenly, I felt a tiny stab of fear about my first day completely alone on the island. Not even Mercedes would be there working to keep me company.

I made my way slowly back to the island, wishing I had gone into town. But I had nowhere to go and knew no one to visit. As I rounded the peninsula, I could see that little white speck on the rocks. Cory was waiting and happy I'd returned so soon.

It was a long day. I read, did some crewel stitching, and baked a cake. We definitely had something to celebrate, and I even heated water and took a bubble bath, made up my face, and tried to fix my hair before I left to get Joe at the dock.

I was so excited to see him by the time he pulled into Asese at five o'clock, it was like the first time we met.

He bounded out of the truck and ran toward me. I threw my arms around his neck as he cried out, "I loved it!"

"You gonna ski home?" I asked.

"Nah," he answered, "I've got too much to tell you!"

He described the little office and how Ramon had purchased all the necessary equipment for him. The meal at noon had been two meats, four or five vegetables (Joe wasn't sure about one of the dishes), and plenty of fresh fruit drinks with ice.

"He's got a cook and two maids, plus a man who does the gardening, cleans the cars, and fixes things around the house!" Joe exclaimed.

"How wonderful!" I shouted as he described everything.

"Oh, Sandy," Joe said as he leaned over and kissed me, "it's so good to have you to come home to. You looked beautiful when I pulled up to Asese."

He made me feel so good. For a few minutes I'd almost been fearful of his newfound joy. For the first time we weren't going to be able to share in the day's labors, and that was going to take some getting used to.

"What was it like having a little privacy?" he asked.

"Oh, it was all right, but I got a little lonely," I admitted.

"If you want you can come with me into town. Ramon's wife insisted you could spend the day at their home if you'd like."

"That's very kind of her, but I wouldn't feel right being there all day."

"Oh, but you would," Joe insisted. "These people really mean it when they say, 'Mi casa es su casa.'"

We enjoyed our supper, and Joe especially appreciated the fresh coconut cake. By the time we had eaten, the lantern had to be lit.

As we listened to HCJB I reflected on what had happened in just a few hours. Just as God had promised in Philippians 4:19, He had supplied all our needs according to His riches in glory by Christ Jesus.

We received a letter the next day from Pedro Chamorro with a copy of the article and the pictures he had taken for the paper. He was enthused about the response his article had received. He also wanted to share with us that his wife had had a baby girl and would love to meet us. Could we have dinner with his family some evening when we were in Managua?

We appreciated his kindness and hoped to accept his invitation soon.

Joe loved his job. Ramon needed some preliminary drawings and a model to take to the bank for a loan to complete his project. Since Joe enjoyed making models as much as drawing, he could hardly wait to go to work each morning.

I must admit I felt a few pangs of jealousy, but I kept them to myself. After all, it would be crazy to be jealous of such a wonderful answer to prayer, wouldn't it? As the days wore on, alone on the island, I knew I was going to have to do something to keep myself busy, or those "pangs" were going to develop into something much worse.

When Joe came home from work a few days later, I mentioned my idea of finding something to do even if it was part-time. I had so wanted to start a school for the island children but knew my Spanish just wasn't good enough to teach—especially to teach reading, writing, and arithmetic in the Spanish language. Besides, when we had spoken with Mercedes and some other island parents, they explained that their children had to work every day so there would be enough food for the family.

It seemed that door had closed.

About the only place I could think of to work was the Embassy school in Managua—the American-Nicaraguan School.

"If it's only part-time a couple of days a week," Joe admitted, "it would give you something to prepare for and would be worth the time to make the trip."

"I think I better try," I said, "because as much as I hate to say it, the island just isn't the same when I'm by myself."

So the next day I went to Managua and asked about working. To my delight, they were looking for someone to have a drama class for some of the elementary children after school one day a week. With my experience and training I was accepted and agreed to begin the next week.

I was so happy as I returned from Managua on Ramon's big green bus. I couldn't wait to tell Joe of my new job.

I shared my news joyfully. He finished gluing a tiny piece of wood on a model and then hugged me.

"It seems everything works out for those who love the Lord," he agreed.

As we headed home that evening, we sang at the top of our lungs. We were truly discovering paradise!

NINETEEN

Time to Enjoy

The next day, October 27, was my birthday and our ten-month anniversary. Ramon had invited me to spend the day at his home, for he and his wife wanted to take Joe and me out to eat in celebration.

That morning, I packed a totebag of makeup, hair curlers, books, and clothes. I wanted to look extra special for our night out. *Besides,* I thought, *today is my twenty-fourth birthday, and I'm finally discovering the reasons I was born—to praise God and enjoy His creation.*

"You wanna ski in?" Joe asked as I brushed my hair back and clasped it off my neck.

I thought for a moment and decided there was no reason I shouldn't. So I was the one who waved at our little island friends that beautiful October morning.

I put on a skirt and top in the back of the truck, and we were soon in Granada at Ramon's house. Joe kissed me good-by and ran around the block to the hardware store just as the doors were being unlocked for business.

I walked into the huge stucco house with the open center courtyard and noticed some beautiful flowers arranged on a table. There was a card that caught my eye because on it was written, "A Sandy."

"Are these for me?" I exclaimed as Maria Elena came from their bedroom.

"*Feliz cumpleaños,*" she said as her son and daughter emerged from their rooms and called out the same birthday greeting.

"*Gracias,*" I answered as she showed me to a room with a bath where I could relax and do whatever I pleased for the whole day.

A huge painting of a beautiful young woman was hanging in the room. "*Es mamá,*" little Maria Amanda, age five, told me as I stared at it.

I learned that Maria Elena was a former Miss Nicaragua and had represented her country at the Miss Universe pageant years earlier. Her daughter was a doll and entertained me with little Spanish poems complete with perfect gestures.

Their son, Ramon, Jr., was seven years old and adored his little sister. He showed me his toys and his bike-riding skills.

The house was huge, with a center courtyard surrounded by a tile patio—a perfect place for the children to play with no danger of being hurt in the street.

At about noon, Ramon and Joe showed up for lunch. We sat down at the huge, formal dining table and enjoyed a delicious meal. Then, Ramon excused himself for his afternoon siesta. Joe explained that most of the people did this. Because of the intense mid-day heat, just about every business in town was closed until two in the afternoon.

We went upstairs to a balcony overlooking the city and stretched out in a hammock. After the big meal, I was asleep in seconds.

Then, the men went back to work, and I got ready for the evening out. Maria Elena told me about *El Club Jockey* and I was eager to eat there. That was one of the first places I'd noticed when we entered Granada for the first time, and I'd always admired the beautiful white buildings and carefully landscaped lawns.

Before we left for dinner, the Lopez family generously presented me with several little gifts. I was thrilled and overwhelmed with their generosity. I had been so afraid that my birthday would be just another day that I had dreaded it, but now I thanked God for His goodness. My mother had always gone overboard at birthdays and Christmas. I had wondered what a birthday away from home would be like, but my fears had been ungrounded.

The meal was fabulous. Seafood with all the trimmings made it one of the most memorable meals of my life. Ramon and Maria Elena made me feel as if I were with family.

Joe and I drove back to Asese late that night. We weren't sure if we could find our way home in the dark or not, but we needed to get to the island.

"I think I can make it," Joe said as we peered out into the darkness.

It was a new moon, and there wasn't much light as we stepped into the boat. It had been such a wonderful evening I didn't really worry about getting home.

We set out into the dark, murky waters. After a while it was apparent we were not exactly where we wanted to be. Nothing looked familiar in the darkness.

Joe had the engine just barely putting along. We were both scanning the water trying to see into the darkness for hidden boulders.

"Why didn't we just stay at the dock tonight?" I finally asked in desperation.

"No fair!" Joe said. "That's Monday morning quarterbacking. Now that we're out here, let's not start wishing we'd done something else."

My eyes were feeling strained as I peered into the waters. "Look out to the right!" I shouted as Joe quickly maneuvered the boat around a sharply pointed rock jutting up from the water.

We didn't take our eyes off the water until I noticed how close Mombacho seemed to loom above us. "Uh-oh," I said, "I think we've done it again."

"What?" Joe asked without taking his eyes off the water.

"We've veered too far to the west like we did months ago when we were caught in the afternoon wind." I pointed upward at the cloud-covered mountain.

Just as Joe turned the boat toward the east we saw a light on an island about half a mile away. "Maybe we should head for the light," he offered.

So we went slowly on toward the light. As we approached, we could hear someone whistle, and then we saw another light on another island further east. Out went the light we'd been following.

"What could it mean?" I asked in confusion.

"I don't know, but I'm going toward the light," Joe answered. "At least I know our island is east, and we're getting closer."

On and on we motored, but when we got close to the light again we heard a whistle, and further on was another light flickering in the darkness.

"They're signaling us!" Joe shouted.

"What?" I said incredulously.

"It has to be!" he went one. "The islanders recognize our boat motor and know we're in the wrong direction, so they're leading us back home."

I laughed as I realized he was exactly right. I gave a loud "OWwhoop!" and the person holding the next lantern whistled back. Joe whistled and steered us on through the darkness.

As soon as we neared the next lantern, another would light up on across the lake. We followed their lights until we suddenly began to recognize the familiar outline of the peninsula and knew we were almost home.

We finally arrived and Cory meowed her welcome. As we climbed into bed, I hoped to thank all our friends who had helped us, but we never did learn who they were.

In the coming weeks we were busy. Joe loved working for Ramon, and I looked forward to the drama class in Managua. We learned that our home country had a new president named Jimmy Carter and wondered about the man from Georgia who made the headlines of *La Prensa* with the words, *born again*. He had the whole country talking.

Joe and I made a trip into Managua to visit with the young editor, Pedro Chamorro, and his wife. When we arrived at their home, we were greeted by a maid. I wondered how a "struggling young editor" could afford such a beautiful home with a central courtyard. "This is my mother and father's room," he said pointing to a beautiful suite of rooms off the central courtyard, "and there are my brother and sister's quarters."

I realized that he still lived with his parents. On one side of the home they had built a little apartment for him and his wife. The whole house was charming and we felt welcome.

Then he insisted that we have supper with them. As we sat down at the table, we were introduced to his family. His father seemed very preoccupied but was courteous and told us he had enjoyed the article about us.

Joe was answering questions and tried to change the subject to learn a little about this cordial family. "And what do you do, Sr. Chamorro?" Joe asked.

The man stopped eating and stared at us as if he hadn't understood the question. Joe asked him again, and he grinned. I looked at Joe and he looked at me. Had he asked the wrong question?

Pedro spoke up with a chuckle, "Didn't you know? My father owns *La Prensa!*"

I could feel my face turning red, and Joe gently tapped my foot with his own. We felt like idiots!

We tried to finish our meal, but it was difficult to eat as we tried to listen closely to every word spoken around that table. Here we sat with a man who had suffered much for freedom of the press.

As we finished eating, a number of distinguished-looking gentlemen arrived at the home for a meeting of some sort. As we left the table, we apologized for our ignorance and thanked Pedro's mother, Doña Violeta, for the lovely meal.

We walked with Pedro back to his apartment. His wife spoke no English and retired to their bedroom to be with their new baby daughter. Joe and I learned a lot about this interesting family, and for the first time we realized that the beautiful, gentle people of Nicaragua were feeling the first tremors of a much greater problem than any earthquake had ever caused. Beneath the surface of this friendly society, there were rumblings of discontent with the present government, and a few individuals were boldly proclaiming their dissatisfaction. Pedro Chamorro was one of them.

As we left, Pedro promised to come for another visit to *El Corazón* and hoped to get some fishing done. We waved good-by and climbed into our truck.

I let the knowledge of the Chamorros' company sink in. "That was probably the most influential man in Nicaragua besides President Somoza!"

"And to think," Joe said, "that every one of these people coming for that meeting could be discussing something that could change every Nicaraguan's way of life."

We rode along in silence for a long time, letting the conversations of the evening replay in our minds.

"You know what?" I asked. "We never even got to tell them how God has been our strength through our endeavor on the island."

"I know," Joe admitted. "I kept wanting to say something, but didn't quite know how to put it in front of a man like that."

"Isn't it crazy?" I stated. "Why don't we have the boldness to speak about our Lord?"

We both felt very frustrated as we pulled into Asese and climbed into the camper for the night. "Oh, God," Joe prayed before we went to sleep, "please help Sandy and me speak up for You when we know we should. Forgive us if we offended You. We would never have made it this far without You!"

We didn't have as much time in the coming weeks to study, but we were reading the book of Acts and trying to figure out the change in the disciples after Jesus ascended to heaven. Making time for our study was a struggle, and the arrival of our eleven-month anniversary meant Christmas would be around the corner. Our studying had to wait.

I was getting so excited about the prospect of going back to Tennessee for a visit, I was beside myself. Everything I planned was for our trip home. I made myself a new skirt, some slacks and a vest, and a new top on my treadle sewing machine. Joe was busy as ever working for Ramon and we were watching our pennies, whoops, I mean centavos, in order to fly home for the holidays.

Since the *Prensa* article, we had been invited to a whole new set of "island people's" places. Many private businessmen owned islands and would send after us on Saturday and Sunday afternoons to visit with them and their families. We were amazed how some of the islands had been developed.

One man was one of the first registered architects in Nicaragua and was rightfully proud of his beautiful island. There were several little bungalows, all with electricity! He had a generator housed in a building away from the main living area so we couldn't hear the sound.

Living on *El Corazón* all those months, surrounded only by islanders, I had certainly never imagined that just around the peninsula were all these weekend retreats.

The next weekend we decided to get away from the curious visitors who kept dropping in each Saturday and Sunday. I packed a picnic lunch and we headed for Asese. We had decided it was long past time that we went up on top of Mombacho to gain a new perspective on our island paradise.

We drove several kilometers south of Granada and turned up a dirt road leading up the mountain. All along the winding way were huge plantations where landscaping plants were being cultivated. Nearer the top we had to park at a huge *finca* where coffee was grown. We watched an old man and several young boys spreading the beans on a huge expanse of concrete to dry in the sun.

We walked up through the forest until we reached a clearing to see the lake. What a sight it was! The islands looked like tiny green gems dotting the lake's surface. And there in the heart of the whole archipelago was our little jewel, *El Corazón*.

We drove home late that afternoon in great satisfaction. So much had happened in eleven months! We would never have grown so fast or found such peace without our commitment to God and faith in His Word.

The next morning Joe drove off in the boat, and I hurried to get the house cleaned up and begin sewing. We were so busy getting ready to go to Tennessee that I didn't have time to get homesick—especially not since we were going to be there in just a few more days.

We made Christmas gifts for our families, including handmade mahogany commode seats. Finally in the last few days, we made arrangements for two Peace Corps couples we had met to come out and spend several days on the island while we were gone. Mercedes' children agreed to bring Cory a live fish each afternoon, and we promised them some Christmas treats when we returned.

The morning of December sixteenth I felt as nervous as I had on our wedding day. It had been almost a year since I'd seen my family. Joe and I had changed so much—would the same be true of our families? Soon we would see.

We waited at the Managua International Airport for our flight that would take us in just two short hours back into the homeland we had left a year earlier. Of all days for delays, that had to be the day. Our plane was twelve hours late, the air-conditioning system broke down in the airport, and we began to wonder if we'd ever get back to Tennessee.

Finally, at ten P.M. we were taxiing down the runway. When we set down at Miami International Airport two hours later, I wanted to kiss the ground.

The next two weeks were a blur of questions and visiting in a world that was moving too fast.

As we stepped into my parents' home, I couldn't believe how elegant everything looked. Never had I noticed how "rich" we really were. I walked into the living room and stared at the plush furnishings, the luxury of beautifully painted walls, carpeted floors, and soft, comfortable chairs. I sank down into one for the first time since I'd left home.

Then Joe and I went up to my old bedroom. There was my dressing room just as I'd left it—well, almost as I'd left it. One of my brothers had added his own assortment of school memorabilia. I turned on the faucet and stared at the rush of clean water.

Joe stepped out of the bathroom and said, "Can you believe that we actually flush drinking water down a commode in this country?"

And the lights! Everywhere there were lights. We couldn't even see the stars for the brightness of the streets with everyone's Christmas decorations aglow.

It was baffling to hear people discussing TV shows we'd never even heard of. How unimportant the discussions seemed. We wanted to tell everyone we met what had happened during that short year on the island but found ourselves floundering for words. Life for our families and friends had gone on as usual, but it seemed to us that we had stepped into another time zone, and they couldn't comprehend the deep changes that had taken place within us.

By the end of the vacation, I was looking forward to returning to the island but also dreading leaving my family again—as well as the luxury of modern conveniences. I felt confused and didn't know what I really wanted.

Saying good-by to those we loved so much was even more difficult than the first time. Now I knew where we were going and what lay ahead for me on the island, and I wasn't that sure I wanted to return. Joe sensed my apprehension and tried to assure me.

"You'll be fine once we're back on the island and you find work to keep you busy," he said. "God will still take care of us. He hasn't changed just because we've been on vacation!"

I wanted to laugh at his point, but couldn't. It did seem we had left God on the island for the hustle and bustle of the two weeks we'd been home.

We waved good-by to our families at the airport and boarded the plane with tears streaming down our faces. Again we sought God's protection over them and us in our separation.

Just eight hours later we had traveled from freezing cold to tropical heat. Managua's streets were teeming with traffic as we searched for a bus to take us to Granada.

My shoulders ached with the luggage and gifts we'd brought. We crossed the hot pavement to the shade of some trees and waited.

Finally a bus heading for our destination pulled over. As we stepped into the bus, the driver smiled and greeted us warmly. "Joe y Sandy?" he asked in recognition.

We nodded in surprise. Then another man said he'd read about us in *La Prensa* and really liked the article.

We staggered down the crowded aisle to the back of the bus. A chicken squawked as Joe pushed by a woman whose live produce was hanging out in the aisle.

"It's great to be back, huh?" I laughed. We fell into a seat as the bus lurched ahead.

Several young men in school uniforms sat around us. They stared at me until one of them said, "Hey, I know where I've seen them—in *La Prensa!* You two are the ones who found your paradise in the islands!"

They began to ask questions as we swayed down the highway. It was good to be home.

We finally arrived in Granada, and Joe left me at the depot and walked the few blocks to Ramon's house to let him know we were back. We hoped to borrow his car to go on to Asese so we could get back to the island.

I drew several curious stares as I sat on our suitcase among all our luggage and bags of gifts. Finally, Joe and Ramon pulled up, and we piled in the car for the few kilometers out to Asese.

The sun was setting over Ometepe, an active volcano to the southwest. I could see a puff of black smoke wafting upward in the afternoon wind.

Joe hurriedly loaded the boat and told Ramon he'd be at work the following day. Then we were off across the lake, the familiar palm trees waving from the shore as we glided along. At the sound of our motor the children of the dancing island scampered out and waved, too. We sped on to Mercedes' island because we couldn't wait to deliver our gifts.

Despite all the gifts and joy we had shared with our families during the holidays, the islanders made our Christmas that year. As we dispensed each family member a brightly wrapped gift, they examined the packages closely. There was no desperate tearing to get inside and see the contents. They just stared at the paper and ribbons.

"I don't believe they know to open them," I whispered to Joe as we took their pictures.

Joe encouraged them to look inside and they very carefully removed the wrappings one at a time so everyone could enjoy what everyone else had received. I could feel my eyes filling with tears as the little children opened theirs and found dolls they'd only dreamed of and a toy boat for "Little Mercedes."

Later, as we motored the last mile to the island, I allowed my tears to fall. Just as we docked at El Corazón, Cory ran to us—for the first time—instead of scampering away after we greeted her.

Mercedes and his family had worked diligently keeping Cory fed and watching out for the island. They had even cleaned the whole house while we were gone.

The floors shone, everything had been dusted, and the water tank was full of water!

"We're blessed!" Joe said as we got into bed.

I had to agree.

TWENTY

Revelation and Revolution

The next few weeks were difficult for me. The anticipation of seeing our families, the maddening rush at Christmas, and then the return to the island was all behind us. The excitement was over.

Joe was going to work each day as usual, and I stayed on the island trying to fill the hours with study, needlework, and reading. Those were the longest days of my life. The only thing that kept me from being really depressed was the surprise visits from strangers every few days.

It all began one afternoon when I was preparing our supper. As I took the meat from the refrigerator and began to cut it into bite-sized pieces, I distinctly heard my inner voice say, "Better make more than you had planned."

Without even questioning this suggestion, I cut up more meat for the Chinese dish I was preparing to cook.

A little while later, I had everything ready and walked out to the dock to wait for Joe. I couldn't wait to discuss with him what I had been reading in the book of Acts about the power of the Holy Ghost, but when I saw our boat come speeding around the peninsula, Joe wasn't alone. Two other figures were in the boat with him.

So that's why I needed more food! I laughed to myself. "How wonderful you are, O Lord!"

As Joe parked at our rock pier, I recognized the young couple with him. It was Eric and Donna Stein from Knoxville! We had been acquainted with them at UT, and Eric had been with Joe in the first group of UT students who had come to Nicaragua after the earthquake.

"What in the world are you two doing here?" I asked in amazement. They were actually standing before me on *our* island!

"We just had to come and see you," Donna answered. "Ever since Eric was here as a student he's wanted to come back for a visit and show me the country that captured his heart. So here we are." She was already walking up the stone steps to the house. "Praise God," I heard her say. "It's so beautiful!"

I couldn't believe my ears. Did I hear what I thought I heard? The last time I'd talked with Donna, she was kind of unsettled and was searching for answers in all the wrong places. Now she was praising the Lord.

I looked at Joe and read his lips as he said soundlessly, "You won't believe it!"

We followed them up the steps and Joe lit the lantern before we settled down for supper.

"I hope we're not putting you guys out or anything," Eric said in his quiet way.

"Oh, no," I insisted. "I just had a feeling that Joe might have visitors with him tonight."

Donna looked at me and smiled a radiant smile. "The Lord told you, didn't He?" she asked and waited for me to reply.

"Why . . . uh," I stammered, "yes, but . . ."

Donna nudged Eric and laughed. "I told you we were supposed to come on out here," she said.

I looked at her. What had happened to this woman who had been so mixed up when we were in school? The glazed look I remembered seeing in those confused blue eyes had been replaced by a radiant glow. Her eyes sparkled with joy.

Joe asked the blessing, and we talked over old times as we ate. He and I could hardly take our eyes off Donna and Eric. Something had definitely changed their lives, and we would hear all about it at the proper time.

After they helped with dishes, telling us how they had decided to come to Nicaragua for a vacation, we all settled down around the lantern. Joe offered Eric the hammock, Donna and I sat in our only two chairs, and Joe sat on a pillow on the floor.

We told them about our first year on the island and they listened enthusiastically. Finally, we wanted to hear about what they had been doing for the last two years.

Donna began, "Well, first of all we've become Christians!"

That was obvious, but her boldness amazed us.

We listened to them relate the story of their conversion. Neither of them had attended an organized church as children, yet here they were quoting Scripture as I'd never heard anyone do—not even a preacher.

How can they know so much in such a short time? I wondered. Joe was getting restless, and I could tell he didn't know what to say to them or how to react.

We told them of our decision a few months earlier to accept Jesus Christ as the Lord of our lives and the many times God had answered our prayers, including the time with Mercedes' daughter and then finding work in Granada.

"That's wonderful," Donna said, "and the Holy Spirit has been teaching you directly from the Word, hasn't He? Now, Jesus wants to fill you with His Holy Spirit and give you the power you so desperately need for what is to come!"

"What are you talking about?" Joe asked rather bluntly.

Donna wasn't one bit intimidated as she continued. "You see here," she said as she unpacked a well-worn Bible from her suitcase and sat back down, "in the book of Acts how all the people who believed in Jesus were also filled with His power. He came to baptize you with fire and with power."

I stopped rocking in my chair and stared at her. How was it possible that she would be talking about the very subject I had been studying for the past few days? I couldn't ask enough questions, and she seemed to have an answer for them all. She flipped through the Bible as if she had studied it all her life. The more she talked, the more I wanted what she spoke of.

About midnight Joe insisted we all get some rest. After all, he had to go to work the next day and the rest of us could talk all day long.

When we got into bed I whispered to him. "Joe, what she's telling us about is true. I've been studying all those Scriptures myself and I've been wanting to talk to you about it."

Joe put his hand over my mouth and said, "Shhh!"

I looked at him, and when he uncovered my mouth I said, "What's wrong with you?"

He was certainly agitated by the whole conversation. "I don't know what to believe yet!" he whispered. "Don't you remember how confused Donna was two years ago? We'll talk about it some more after they leave. Now get some sleep!"

I lay there for a long time staring at the stars through our louvered walls, listening to the waves crashing on the rocks and the wind blowing through the coconut palms.

There was no way the events of the day could all be a coincidence. The studying I'd been doing, the inner voice telling me to prepare for guests, the evidence of God's power in Donna's life, and her boldness to share her knowledge with us all added up. I definitely needed this power that she and the Bible spoke of, and I wasn't going to settle for anything less.

"Father," I prayed in silence, "I know You are a great God and have done so many things for Joe and me that we can't even remember them all to thank You. I appreciate Your faithfulness and now am asking You to show me Your perfect will in this matter. You know what the future holds, and if You have a power that we're going to need, I want to find it. Please, help Joe and me in this search. If we start to make mistakes, draw us unto You. I praise You for everything You've blessed us with. In Christ's name, amen."

The next morning Joe and Eric left in the boat at seven A.M. Donna and I cleaned up the dishes and sat down to talk. A thousand questions sprang from my lips that day, and we found the answers to them all. By afternoon I wanted to share this new step of faith with Joe.

"It's all right," Donna assured me. "God has called you two to be a witness to His power."

She spoke with authority, and I was at peace within. I knew she was right.

There was no further discussion when Joe and Eric returned that afternoon. Joe was too busy pointing out places of interest on our map of Nicaragua. Eric and Donna wanted to visit them all.

They left the next day. They wanted to travel around the country so Eric could show Donna why he, too, had fallen in love with this amazing land. "It's true," he admitted when they got in the boat to leave, "once the sand of this land fills your shoe, you will always return."

"We left you a little surprise," Donna said as Joe started the motor. I waved good-by and turned to go back to the house with Cory.

On the counter where we had built book shelves was a tape. I picked it up and looked at the little plastic box. "The Second Chapter of Acts," it said. I put the tape into the player and listened as three young people sang their powerful songs. By the end of the tape, I had no doubts about

God's Holy Spirit. He was a Person who could fill us with power to be like Jesus and lead us in a closer walk with God.

That evening Joe and I went over all the references we could find about the Holy Spirit in the Bible. If the disciples who had been with Jesus daily needed Him, then we did. It was as simple as that. After listening to the music tape, Joe and I both kneeled on our living room floor and asked God to fill us with His power. He did. Little did we know then that it would later become a matter of life or death.

Other surprise visitors graced our home. I learned to make bread from a woman traveling around the world from Canada; a woman from Washington state taught me the art of making jelly; we sailed on a trimaran to Costa Rica one weekend. All of these strangers gave us much in their short visits on the island. Our Heavenly Father sent each one into Joe's path in Granada, and each shared our little paradise.

By the end of February, Joe was almost finished designing the projects for Ramon. We wondered what would happen next.

"I sure hope he'll finish the construction soon," I said one evening as we ate supper. "Then, I'd have a steady job at last, and maybe you could do some freelance work."

"I don't know," Joe said. "It's going to take quite a while to complete the projects and I don't really think there's too much private work for an architect here in Granada."

That night we prayed about the matter before we went to sleep. God had not failed us yet. Why should we not trust Him now?

In the morning, I watched Joe until he was out of sight and felt a strange anticipation as I went back to the house. By afternoon I kept looking at the clock every few minutes, hoping it was almost time for Joe to return from work.

At about four o'clock I heard the drone of our motor heading around the peninsula. I ran to the pier to wait for Joe's arrival. He stood up and danced like a wild man. Something had definitely happened.

"What is it?" I screamed as he cut off the engine.

"Sit down!" he said. He jumped from the boat onto the rocks beside me.

"What, what?" I insisted.

"The current professor for UT in Managua has just resigned!" Joe practically yelled. "They want me to take over the program and live in Managua."

I was excited, yet apprehensive. Could this be the answer to our prayer? I certainly hadn't considered leaving the island especially not moving to Managua. Our living expenses would be tremendous in the capital city. Before I could voice any of my doubts, Joe continued.

"They'll pay all our living expenses, and we'll still be able to come to the island on weekends. There'll be more opportunities for you in Managua, too. What do you think?" he asked breathlessly.

"It sounds too good to be true," I answered. "We'll just have to list all the pros and cons of leaving the island and pray some more."

Within a few days, we knew this was our next step. I began to think of all the advantages of living in Managua: running water, electricity, a cook and a maid, being around other people, job opportunities, and nice vacations every few months when there were university breaks. And of course, we still would have the island. All those things outweighed the negatives: living with ten to fifteen other people, the maddening rush of the city, the sounds and smells of a large metropolis, and the adjustment for Cory. It seemed we were heading toward a new goal—an unknown adventure.

Joe and I adjusted smoothly to the move, but not Cory. She didn't eat for eight days, and after a trip to the veterinarian for shots, worming, and a thorough checkup, she withdrew to our closet and curled up in a pitiful, trembling ball of fur.

"I'm really worried about her," I mentioned to Joe as he came from one of the projects the students were working on.

"She'll be all right," he insisted, but as the days passed, she grew weaker and weaker.

That weekend we took her back to the island with us. She walked slowly up the steps and made her way down into the rocks where she had lived when we first arrived on *El Corazón*.

When it was time to leave, she wouldn't come out to us, so we left a freshly caught fish and a dish of real cat food, asked Mercedes' family to care for her, and left her there.

On Monday morning, a young man from the Peace Corps phoned to ask if he and his new bride could spend a couple of days on the island for their honeymoon.

"Sure," Joe said and gave them directions about the stove, refrigerator, and lantern.

When they returned on Friday morning, the young man came to the villa where we lived with six other students. I heard his voice as the maid answered the door.

"How was the island?" I asked cheerfully.

He looked at me so sadly as he began to speak. "It was fantastic," he began, "but I have some sad news for you."

I looked at him with anticipation. Too many thoughts flooded my head—Mercedes? The Wilsons? Fire?

"Your little cat—" he stammered, "she died the night we got there."

I stared at him in disbelief. Cory, dead? I immediately began to think of the last week in Managua and her refusal to eat.

I was numb. I heard the fellow thanking me. I know I must have said something, but I don't really remember. I walked back through the house to our room, went in and closed the door, flung myself on the bed, and cried. I felt I'd lost a member of our family and it was my fault.

Joe got back from Granada just as the Peace Corps volunteer pulled away from the villa. We were both upset at the loss of our little friend. We had come to think of her as a little angel God had sent us to make the year's work a little easier. I wrote later: "We both get too attached to pets."

But within days we were both wanting another one. They're so much fun—especially on an island. It didn't take long to find one, or rather for one to find us.

A scrawny mutt had been coming by the villa every evening about supper time. He enjoyed the scraps Joe took out to the street for him and all the other street animals.

Two nights after the news of Cory's death, Joe went out to the street with a pork chop bone in his hand. The cinnamon brown dog ran as Joe approached and stood looking at him from a street light halfway down the street. The dog's face said, "No way, José! I've been kicked too many times."

Joe crouched down and waited. Before too long the dog tucked his head down and crept forward. He could smell the pork chop. Joe waited patiently while the animal made his way nearer.

When the dog was within three or four yards of Joe, Joe tossed the pork chop to him. The dog tucked his tail and ran back a few feet, but turned and ran for the bone. Joe repeated this haphazard feeding for over an hour until the dog allowed him to touch him.

Joe walked back into the villa with a look of triumph on his face. "Tomorrow," he announced, "I'll have that dog eating out of my hand."

I didn't doubt it.

Sure enough, the dog was back the next evening, and Joe was ready with some scraps of meat. Within fifteen minutes, the dog was eating from his hand and allowing him to pet him.

"Poor thing!" I said when I saw the dog's protruding ribs.

"He's friendly once he trusts you," Joe said as he stroked the filthy dog.

As the days went by, our visitor gradually knew he could trust the people who lived in our house. He would lie on the porch unless someone came through the door. Then, he would run and hide in the shrubbery.

Finally one night Joe was able to pick him up and carry him back to the concrete shower and sink where the maid did the laundry. He bathed the trembling animal who shook his way out of the house and rolled in the grass outside.

Once he was dry, he frolicked playfully, and we tried to approach him once more. He was our new pet.

The only name that suited our newfound friend was Gringo since that's what we were—foreigners.

We headed for the island that weekend. "If the dog likes the water," Joe announced as we piled into the truck, "he's got a new home."

Gringo lay in the floor of the truck at my feet throughout the drive to Granada. He never moved or whimpered.

Once we got to Asese, Joe opened the door and called, "Come on, boy, you can get out now."

Like a flash of lightning, the dog sprang from the truck. When he caught sight of the water, he ran and leapt out into the lake with a splash and paddled around as if he'd always been a water dog.

"Well," I crowed, "he must understand English very well 'cause he just passed the test that qualified him to be our pet."

Joe was staring at the water and holding his sides with laughter. "What a great dog!"

Gringo hopped into the boat as if he'd always been with us, and we were off. When we were about twenty-five yards from the island, Joe slowed down to watch for rocks. Gringo took that opportunity to leap from the boat and swim the rest of the way!

Once we had unloaded the boat and opened up the house to allow the wind to blow through and cool it off, we headed for the water to swim. Gringo loved our homemade raft, and we played for hours.

That evening we were sitting around the lantern listening to HCJB and reading the latest magazines. I glanced at Joe in the hammock and at the same moment he looked up at me. *"Te amo!"* I said with a big smile. "I love you, too," he winked back. We were enjoying paradise at last.

Suddenly the quiet reverie was shattered. Gringo had been out exploring the island in the darkness. We watched him stumble into the house and collapse at the door. Foam was coming from his mouth. He was trembling all over.

"What could have happened to him?" I cried in desperation. "He was just fine a few minutes ago. Now it looks as if he's dying!"

Joe was kneeling at Gringo's side, stroking him. "Sandy," he commanded, "get something! We've got to get whatever he's eaten out of him!"

I ran to our medicine cabinet. I grabbed anything I could find that I thought would make the dog throw up. I mixed several things together and ran to Joe. "Here!"

"It's impossible to get it in him," Joe cried. "His jaws are locked shut! He's getting stiff!"

"Oh, Joe," I sobbed, "I don't want to lose him. What could have happened to him? Why did we have to bring him here? First, Cory died in the city, and now our new pet is going to die on the island!"

"Don't say that!" Joe demanded. "We've just got to help him." Even Joe was crying now. He loved animals so much it was awful for him to watch the dog suffering.

Gringo was having convulsions, and Joe stood up and walked out the back door. He came back in with the machete.

"What are you going to do?" I sobbed.

"I can't stand here and watch this dog suffer," he cried. "I'm going to put him out of his misery."

I hid my face in my hands and cried. Unexpectedly, I heard that familiar inner voice say: "I shall supply *all* your needs!" "Joe, stop!" I cried out with authority. "Let's pray!"

Joe lowered the machete to his side. The dog lay at his feet. If he was breathing, I couldn't tell. "We've got no other choice. He's almost dead anyway, so what would it hurt?"

We laid our hands on the now still body of our stiff little companion. "Lord," Joe began, "we don't know how to help this poor creature, but You do. Please tell us what to do for him if it is Your will. I pray in Jesus' name. Amen."

"Bring him out to the old table under the water tank," I shouted. "I know it sounds crazy, but we should spray water from the hose into the dog's mouth."

"What good would that do?" Joe asked. "Look at him! He's already dead."

"Come on," I insisted. "If I don't do what I think I should, how will I ever know if God really answered our prayer?"

We carried the stiff body out to the table and put the water hose up to the clenched teeth. As the water sprayed into the dog's mouth, it streamed back out.

"It's no use!" Joe insisted, but suddenly the dog began to breathe. His rib cage was heaving up and down. Within a few seconds more, he was trying to get up.

Joe cried as the dog staggered to his feet. "He's going to live!" He hugged the dog, and we danced around like children as we praised God for His answer to our prayer. Within an hour, Gringo was running around like his normal self.

A few days later in Managua, we were relating the incident to some of the students. One of them was from Florida and said that there are certain types of toads in the tropics that are fatal to animals. If one is bitten its skin oozes a poison that paralyzes its victim, and the animal dies unless it gets prompt attention. "What's the cure for it?" I asked realizing that must be what had happened to Gringo on the island.

"They say," the student answered, "running water full force into the animal's mouth dilutes the poison."

I had had no knowledge of this type of toad, much less a cure if an animal happened to bite into one. Yet, there on an isolated island, God had heard my prayer and given me the antidote. When Joe and I realized how much we could really depend on our Heavenly Father, we knew we'd never hesitate to ask for His help in the future.

Within two weeks I was hired to teach fourth grade at a private Nicaraguan school. My students were bilingual, and the parents were seriously involved in children's activities. It was a joy to work with other Nicaraguans, and I took the opportunity to improve my Spanish. As my principal explained, "It's as if you went to the United States and learned your English in the backwoods of Kentucky! You speak hillbilly Spanish, and you're going to have a hard time relearning it."

I had learned "island" Spanish. Coming from the hills of East Tennessee, I now had Spanish to match my English!

Joe was busy with projects. He loved the work with the students except when some would gripe about the slow pace of Nicaraguan politics. "Settle down," he'd exhort them. "You're in the tropics now."

During the next twenty months, the UT program designed and built low-cost housing, slaughterhouses, churches, and day-care centers. They also offered loads of ideas for development of the earthquake-torn city of Managua.

We even found the ideal use for God's money. It provided a well to furnish water for a small village in the mountains. The people of the town were told it was a gift of God just as Jesus was the well of living water that would never run dry. Also, a brand new home was built for a woman whose husband had abandoned her and her children. There was much to be done in the name of the Lord for the people of Nicaragua— with no strings attached.

Our faith grew on as we encountered people from all walks of life and from all over the world. God answered prayer after prayer as we struggled to combine the active pace of city life with our newfound faith.

And during those months in Managua we were able to share our new home with our families. Our joy overflowed as we took them to all the places we had discovered in Nicaragua.

Then, one muggy day in March of 1978, the nation was thrown into turmoil. Pedro Joaquin Chamorro was assassinated in the desolate blocks of downtown Managua. *La Prensa* published the pictures of his riddled body on the front page for the whole nation to see. It was blamed on the president, Anastasio Somoza, but everyone knew he would be an outright fool to do such a thing.

Joe went straight to the Chamorros' house and found Pedro III walking to his uncle's home to pick up his little girl. "What happened?" Joe asked solemnly as they walked together.

"The world has gone crazy!" Pedro answered in shock and disbelief. "My father was the voice of freedom in Nicaragua, and now he is silent."

TWENTY-ONE

Adios

The next weeks were full of turmoil for our beloved country. Major businesses proclaimed strikes to protest the brutal slaying, and accusations were thrown at the Somozas that had never been voiced before. All eyes of the world were upon Nicaragua.

The rumblings we had sensed months before erupted into an impatient national cry for change. The people felt they had suffered long enough because of the Somoza family and their greed. Revolution became the cry of the masses.

Surely, the Somozas had brought much change for the better in Nicaragua, but perhaps along the way too many people were trampled and used. Now those trampled would get their revenge.

By August of 1978 it was growing increasingly difficult to get to the island each weekend. Somoza had the national guard posted along the way. There was fighting in the mountains as the bands of Sandinistas, as they called themselves, fought to dominate the government.

One morning as Joe and I were preparing to go to work, we felt especially impressed to pray for safety. Rumors were circulating that the Sandinista Liberation Army was going to launch a major offensive against Managua. Joe had to be at the National Palace to pick up some documents that morning, and I was going to school. "Father," Joe prayed as we stood in our bedroom, "please protect Sandy and me today. May we be together this evening."

At about ten A.M. I looked out my classroom window and noticed a number of parents coming to get their children. I watched the administration office for a few minutes and could tell by the activity that something was wrong.

Within minutes, our principal came to each classroom and announced that school would be dismissing early because something had happened at the National Palace—something about a terrorist takeover, hostages, and so on.

Terror gripped me for a second, but then I tried to relax. "Trust me!" said that gentle voice, and I determined to do just that.

The next couple of hours were a maddening struggle to load children into private vehicles and get them home. The highway going by our school had been blocked by the national guard because it was the major thoroughfare in and out of Managua.

We divided the frightened children into groups according to neighborhoods. I loaded a dozen children into the camper behind me and sat four more on the front seat with me. At about noon, we pulled onto the Masaya highway and headed for Managua.

There were numerous roadblocks along the way. The guards were jerking people out of their cars and searching everywhere. I suppose they were looking for guns or, perhaps, revolutionaries. I was trembling as we pulled up to one roadblock, but as we drove up it was if the fellow didn't see us! He was looking at the truck behind us and didn't even motion for us to stop.

I drove on and finally got each child safely home. At about two o'clock, I pulled up to the villa and sat there for a long time, afraid to go in and find out Joe might be among the hostages at the National Palace.

"Oh, Father," I cried, "give me faith to trust You. I know he is in Your protection no matter where he is. Help me not to panic."

As I looked up I saw the UT vehicle swing around the corner of our street. Joe was staring at our truck and hardly parked the vehicle before he was out and running toward me. We hugged each other and thanked God for His care.

"I tried to get to your school, but the roads were blocked," he cried.

"I had to take a lot of the children home," I explained. "I was so worried about you at the National Palace. What's going on?"

"I had just left the place this morning when a big truck pulled up to the front steps," Joe said breathlessly. "There were a whole bunch of what I thought were national guardsmen coming to relieve those on duty, but it turned out to be a group of revolutionaries who took over the place and are still holding the whole cabinet hostage."

"I'm so glad you're not there," I cried clinging to him.

"Me, too, but we must pray for the people in there. I hope no one gets hurt."

The coming hours were very tense as the demands of the group were read over the radio. Within hours President Somoza had paid the ransom requested, and a plane flew the band of men and women to Panama. The revolution was on our back doorstep, and things continued to worsen in the following weeks.

Nicaraguans were demanding that their president resign and a bipartisan junta be appointed to take over the affairs of the country.

With the increasing violence, martial law was declared, and Joe and I knew our time in our new home was drawing to a close. If we couldn't move freely from Managua to the island, we had no desire to remain.

As the fighting drew closer to the capital and Somoza's strength continued to decline, the university program was terminated. It was no longer safe or feasible for students to work and complete their projects.

With much sadness, Joe and I finished our work and made one last trip to *El Corazón*. By that time, we had a squawking scarlet macaw and a gentle little green parrot along with Gringo. As we drove those few kilometers to Granada for that last time, tears filled our eyes.

We visited the Wilsons and told them of our plans to return to the USA. Then, we went to see Mercedes and his family for the most difficult parting we've ever experienced.

He followed us in a dugout as we made our way to the island. We talked for hours into the night. Though Mercedes was illiterate and might be considered uninformed by most, he knew what he didn't want for his homeland. "Yes," he said in Spanish, "I'll admit our lives could be better as far as material things, but at least we are free to speak, to worship as we please, to raise our children in the best way we know. We are a proud people. A happy people! We do not want our liberty taken away."

We prayed with him that night. Nicaragua's hope lay in people like himself and their love of freedom. But to maintain that freedom would require much more than love.

On Sunday afternoon, we cleaned up the house one last time. Mercedes and Rosa Elena stood on the rock pier waiting as we turned to look at our "dream come true" once more.

We walked down the steps toward them and handed them the key to the back door. "It's yours!" Joe said with tears in his eyes, *"Hasta mañana!"*

Mercedes and Rosa Elena were crying, too. They'd never had a real home. They'd been squatters on someone else's land for all their married lives.

"A gift from the Lord," I stammered as I hugged each one of them.

We stepped into the boat, and Gringo jumped in beside us. The two parrots sat on the backs of the seats holding on with all their strength as we pulled away.

Mercedes and Rosa Elena stood on the rock pier hugging one another as we motored slowly away. If we ever returned for a visit all would be cared for.

"Surely," I sobbed, "we'll see them again."

We waved until we were almost around the peninsula. Then Joe cut off the motor and let the boat turn around so we could gaze at our little island one last time.

"We came here in search of a dream," he said as he pulled me into his arms.

"And we discovered the One who made it paradise," I added.

"Adios!" we cried and turned toward a new life.

EPILOGUE

"What are we going to do?" I asked Joe as we bumped along the last few miles in Mexico. We'd been traveling for two weeks, and our anticipation was growing as we approached our homeland. But we still hadn't decided our next course of action.

"Maybe I should go back to school and get my master's degree," Joe replied as we swerved around a herd of cattle. The Mexican cowboy waved gingerly as we passed. "I've enjoyed teaching this last eighteen months, and I'll certainly need an advanced degree if I do that."

I stared at the long, dusty road stretching before us. All I had thought about for several weeks was coming home, settling down near family, and starting our own family. "But you know how much I want children," I reminded him. "Can we at least live near Kingsport?" My mind whirled with the constant packing and unpacking we would go through every Christmas when we visited our families. I could well imagine the additional hassles we'd have with children. I rationalized that if we moved close enough for grandparents to visit us, maybe we could continue to vacation by ourselves.

An inner prompting interrupted my selfish thoughts. "Whatever you think is best for our future," I blurted out.

Finally we arrived at the USA border on a warm, blustery day in November. We thanked God for bringing us this far safely. Gringo stood in the seat between us with his chin resting on the dash. He watched the constantly flowing traffic as we pulled up to the customs office.

Several hours and officials later, Joe and I walked a few blocks to a beautiful motel. Lucy and Lorita would be spending the night in the back of the truck inside the customs compound. Since parrots can carry a disease that is devastating to chickens, we had to wait for the federal veterinarian to inspect them the next morning.

"What luxury!" I shouted from the tubful of bubbles and hot water later that evening. It was difficult to believe we were finally home. As I closed my eyes and lay back to soak, I saw Mercedes and Rosa Elena standing on the dock at *El Corazón*. Tears flooded my cheeks at the thought of the people we had left behind.

Just forty-eight hours later I was gripping the door handle as we sped along the Houston freeways. I hadn't seen traffic like this in three years. Gringo was standing as usual between us and never took his eyes off the road. Every once in a while we could hear Lucy and Lorita squawking from the camper behind us.

A long, sleek camping trailer caught my eye as we drove east on Interstate 10 toward New Orleans. I stared at it as we passed them. *Why not?* I asked myself and reminded Joe of our conversation days ago.

At first we had joked about the idea of living in a camper, but the more we discussed the idea, the more appealing it became. "We'll look at some as soon as we get to Tennessee," Joe said enthusiastically.

We had promised to call home when we arrived in New Orleans. I was trembling with excitement when I heard my dad's voice. "We made it!" I shouted into the phone in our motel room. "Just a few more days and we'll be home."

Dad's voice sounded tense as he congratulated us and told us everyone was fine at home. I sensed something was wrong and motioned for Joe to share the phone. He held his ear close to mine as Dad continued, "We got a letter from Mr. Wilson. He wrote it just two days after you left Nicaragua."

The first thing that entered my mind was Bea. In fact, Joe and I both mouthed her name to each other, thinking perhaps she had died.

"There's bad news," Dad said. "Mercedes is dead."

Our hearts jumped into our throats.

"What?" I cried into the phone, "I . . . I don't think we heard you!"

"It's Mercedes," Dad replied. "He got some kind of poisoning from drinking some homemade alcohol and tried to doctor himself. Rosa Elena couldn't get him to the hospital in time."

Joe and I sat there, the phone pressed to our tear-soaked cheeks. *Why?* The question pounded in our heads.

We finally said good-by and fell back on the bed in the motel room. Neither of us could speak for a long time.

How could we ever have imagined we'd never see him again as we waved farewell just days ago? Could we have somehow prevented this needless death? What more could we have shared with him about God and His Son Jesus?

The rest of the trip home was clouded by Mercedes' death. We wanted answers as we read the Bible each night. We even fantasized that it was all a horrible mistake—that Len was wrong, had just gotten mixed up. But we knew better. Gradually we came to accept the reality of our good friend's death and tried to figure out a way to convey our sympathy to his family.

Their immediate need would be the income lost by his death, so we sent a certified check in care of Ramon Lopez for the amount that Mercedes would have earned for a whole year—just five hundred dollars—and a letter that Ramon could read to them. It seemed like so little, but it was the only thing we could think of to help them.

Our first few weeks at home seemed to pass in a whirlwind. Joe was accepted to graduate school at the University of Florida. We bought a thirty-one-foot camping trailer that seemed beyond any luxury we'd had in Nicaragua. Christmas came and went, and suddenly we were living in Gainesville, Florida. Joe attended classes all day, and I worked for the Office of Student Services in the Alcohol Abuse Prevention Program. Mercedes was often on my mind as I typed reports for Dr. Gonzalez.

The newspaper was filled with headlines about Nicaragua daily. The fighting had intensified, and it was obvious Somoza would have to resign or risk being killed.

Finally, on July 17, 1979, the Sandinistas marched in victory through the streets of Managua. Neither Joe nor I knew what to think. From our observations in Nicaragua, reform was desperately needed, and we hoped this revolution would finally give Nicaraguans freedom and basic human rights. But we also knew the danger of revolution without true repentance and submission to a perfect power.

After all, it had taken the miracle of rebirth for a man and woman who loved each other to live together on a tiny island. How much more do the individuals of a nation need to experience the redeeming grace of God through His Son Jesus Christ and to be filled with the power to love through His Holy Spirit?

"What *will* happen to Nicaragua?" I asked Joe one evening as we read the paper.

"Of course, we can't answer that," Joe replied, "but I do hope Nicaraguans will demand their liberties no matter what the price. It would be a disaster if another handful of greedy, self-serving leaders got in power and ruled with an iron hand. The love and determination of those beautiful people could be crushed into apathy."

"And only God can know the course Nicaragua or any nation will choose," I said thoughtfully, "and only the people of that nation can choose."

I knew we had made the right choice four years earlier on *El Corazón*. If it had not been for the Lord, we could never have become one—with each other, with Him, and now with His creation.

Upon completion of Joe's master's degree, we moved to Kingsport and built a home near family and friends. Joe had fallen in love with building construction and wanted to be able to design and build, so he began working for a construction firm. I had the opportunity to teach Bible in the schools of Kingsport, and we began working on another dream—a house on the side of a hill looking toward North Carolina on one side and Virginia on the other.

Now I sit in that dream. It's 1985, and there are still more dreams to come. We have not yet been blessed with our own children, but we have met many challenges while taking care of foster children who share our home. The sea still beckons, and Joe's dream of owning a sailboat has never diminished over the years. I suppose that will be next.

What has become of our dear friends in Nicaragua? We have stayed in touch, and in many ways island life is unchanged.

Ramon Lopez has opened the resort hotel Joe designed in Granada and at last report is doing a thriving business.

Rosa Elena has remarried and added several more children to her proud family. They still reside on El Corazón and we hope to see them when we visit Nicaragua in 1986.

After fifteen years on the island, Bea Wilson made a final visit back to the United States to see her children and grandchildren. After she returned to Nicaragua, Mr. Wilson found she had died in her sleep one morning before Christmas in 1983.

Mr. Wilson has since remarried. His new wife, Concepción, is an island woman, and we could see during their recent visit to Tennessee that her Christian love had softened Mr. Wilson's heart. As they worshipped with our church in Kingsport and were blessed with generous donations of clothing for their Nicaraguan friends, Mr. Wilson was overcome by the unique love of the Christian community and accepted Jesus Christ as his Savior.

Pedro Chamorro and his young family are self-exiled in Costa Rica to protest the censorship of "La Prensa." His brother and an uncle run the other two national newspapers and espouse the philosophy of the current government. As Pedro says, "They are still my family and when we're together we just don't discuss politics."

We also have remained in contact with Andy and Barbara Grayston, whose daughters are nearly grown now. Each year they manage to drop in for a visit on their way to Disney World.

Nicaragua is not the home we left behind. We want to think that Nicaragua is finally becoming her own country and that Nicaraguans have more freedom than ever before, but the controls sanctioned by their new leaders in the name of completing the revolutionary process make that seem unrealistic.

We want to think that most Nicaraguans can now read and enjoy better health, but we wonder if they can choose what to read and can freely enjoy that good health.

We want to think that greed has been abolished and that at last all people of Nicaragua share equally, but I know too well that Somoza's property is used by another minority and recall that it was a native woman with only one dress, a dirt-floor hut, and eight children who taught me true contentment and sharing.

We want to think that the new leaders of Nicaragua are selfless men who want only what is best for Nicaragua, but we know from our own lives that only God can make selfless men and women.

Sometimes we want to think that there's nothing we can do about Nicaragua anyway—so why think about it at all? But we must because our Heavenly Father continually reminds us to intercede for that fair nation and pray for a true revolution in Jesus Christ.

After all we've been through—the struggles, the homesickness, the culture shock, the death to self—we are grateful that our life with God began with an island.